The Garden
in Bloom

The Garden in Bloom

Ann Lovejoy

Plants & Wisdom
for the Year-Round Gardener
in the Pacific Northwest

SASQUATCH BOOKS
SEATTLE

To the goddess Flora

Printed in the United States of America.
Distributed in Canada by Raincoast Books Ltd.
02 01 00 99 98 5 4 3 2 1

Cover design: Karen Schober
Interior design and composition: Kate Basart
Copy editor: Rebecca Pepper
Indexer: Sigrid Asmus

Library of Congress Cataloging in Publication Data
Lovejoy, Ann, 1951–
The garden in bloom : plants & wisdom for the year-round
gardener in the Pacific Northwest / Ann Lovejoy.
p.   cm.
Includes index.
ISBN 1-57061-139-4
1. Gardening—Northwest, Pacific. I. Title.
SB453.2.N83L674   1998

635.9'09795—dc21   97-44116

Sasquatch Books
615 Second Avenue
Seattle, Washington 98104
(206) 467-4300
books@sasquatchbooks.com
http://www.sasquatchbooks.com

*Sasquatch Books publishes high-quality adult nonfiction and children's books related
to the Northwest (Alaska to San Francisco). For more information about our titles,
contact us at the address above, or view our site on the World Wide Web.*

CONTENTS

INTRODUCTION

Looking back over the past dozen years, I find myself amazed at several things. First of all, my own accidental career never ceases to astonish me. Years ago, when the children were so small, gardening saved my sanity and restored my soul to health. Writing about gardening and sharing the insights and experiences it brought me felt almost as good as the real thing. By passing on what I was learning, I could contribute to the same exhilarating, joyful, healing process in other lives. I never intended to make a career of this love of my life, but somehow a career has happened, and I must say, it's kind of fun. As I explore what it means to be a business, I am discovering a whole range of skills and talents I had no idea I could ever develop. If those of us who have lived this electrifying experience can encourage other women to push past their own perceived limitations, the world will be changed, and very much for everyone's good.

What's more, it feels terrific to be able to use my accumulating if still modest influence to make wonderful projects happen, both for myself and for others. Recently, I opened a garden school in my own backyard. I am teaching lots of classes myself, but others will showcase talented garden makers from all over the region. The ongoing classes will be soundly practical, involving hands-on basics like planting, dividing, and so forth in the garden setting. Design workshops will explore various facets of this varied field, from paths and patios to color work and themed gardens. A border building class will create gardens from drawing plans to planting. In addition, a monthly lecture series will offer both information and inspiration. If that's not enough, people can relax by studying Tai Chi (a martial art and moving meditation), yoga, and chi kung (a Chinese breathing and healing art) in the garden setting. It has been my privilege to assist (usually in a very small way) the rising star of quite a few writers, illustrators, designers, gardeners, and nurseryfolk. All of them were and are extremely talented, able, and deserving people who needed only a tiny boost to get up and running. I look back to the day, so long ago now, when Steve Lorton of *Sunset* magazine came up to my door and said, "Who *are* you and *what* are you doing?" He urged me to start writing, and told me where to send whatever I came up with. That led me up a new branch in my garden path, one which brought me to an exciting present and a hopeful future. If I can do the same for anyone, I am thrilled to have that opportunity.

Steve always says he didn't really do anything, but that's kind of the point. Sometimes, all it takes to set us free is a kindly word of truthful praise, a thoughtful appraisal of our abilities, or encouragement to trust our talents. Our mentors, advisers, and friends can't give us anything we don't have except information, but the greatest gift we can offer each other is a mirror.

In that spirit, I want to share some observations about how our gardens have changed over the past decade or so. For years now, I have been visiting gardens all over the Pacific Northwest, traveling frequently from California's Bay Area to British Columbia. What I am seeing these days excites me to the bone, for it represents an incredible leap in knowledge, understanding, vision, and self-confidence. Years ago, most gardens were of the minimalist, *Sunset* school, in which a tidy appearance and low maintenance were the ruling principles. As the hunger for perennials grew, a lot of gardens changed a lot. During the perennial boom period, the most prevalent model was English. Many people were trying hard to reproduce either the gay, informal cottage style or the billowing borders seen in estate gardens.

More recently, something exciting has started to happen. The extended plant palette now widely available encouraged colorist trends that first copied, then went beyond the English models.

Playful interpretations of many styles created new takes on traditional schools and new schools that are still evolving. For the first
time, English gardens are being overtly influenced by northwestern ones. Right now in England, our woodsy, naturalistic gardens have triggered a spate of—perhaps imitations is not the right
word, but let's say enthusiastic emulations. In 1989, Christopher
Lloyd toured a cluster of cutting-edge gardens in the Bay Area,
then went home, ripped out his rose garden, and began experi
menting with tropicalismo, using plants he has grown for years but
in a refreshingly different manner. Great gardeners like Lloyd,
Rosemary Verey, and Penelope Hobhouse find a lot to admire in
our gardens, and rightly so.

Unbound by tradition, free to experiment, explore, and express
a new way of relating to and interacting with plants, we are pushing
the envelope of garden making. It's very obvious that audiences at
horticultural lectures and workshops are more sophisticated, more
freethinking, and more interested in ideas and visions than in the
past. Just a few years ago, the standard lecture request involved
lists of plants. Now people want to know not so much what to do
with them as what might be done.

I see these and other changes adding up to a story—the coming
of age of a region of gardeners. Our inventive, questing, question-
ing ways are putting the Pacific Northwest firmly on the horticultural map for the rest of the world. Indeed, we are now trendsetters
for the whole country, watched by growers and buyers, our taste
and proclivities eagerly observed and followed. People want to
know what colors we think are cool, what plants we are using,
and what we are doing with them. Northwestern gardeners have
launched trends for tropicalismo, Pacific Rim, neo-colorist, and naturalistic gardening, and other regionally popular concepts are gathering strength as well. We are experiencing firsthand one of the
most exciting periods and places in the entire history of gardening,
and I for one am honored to be a part of what you all are creating.

JANUARY

Ring in the New

January

Like most gardeners, I'm a firm believer in celebration. Almost any event or occasion can be taken as an excuse both to make merry and to be consciously grateful together. The first flower on the hardy cyclamen, the first bright bells on the nodding hellebores, the first spangle of stars on the winter jasmine, all are cause for shared pleasure and appreciation.

The mystic philosopher-musician Abbess Hildegard of Bingen told her flock back in 1142 that people were cast out of the original garden for ingratitude, and that being properly grateful was the way back. At Christmastide, I always listen to her music, notably an album of medieval hymns and prayers called *A Feather on the Breath of God*.

Clear and colorless (in the modern sense), the voices weave a net of wonder. Praise song is properly empty of the gloopier emotions, full instead of a welling gratitude. Hildegarde's offers a genuine delight in what *is*, rather than a plea for the provision of what is not.

For gardeners, this kind of gratitude comes easily. Who can walk unmoved through the garden in any season, surrounded by such astonishing beauty and such generously flowing abundance? Even in winter we can find innumerable signs of life and change. Here a new shoot, there a fallen seedpod producing a thick fur of green sprouts.

Perhaps, for those with eyes to see, there is even more to be found than that. All my life, even as a young child, I have searched the winter garden for signs of spring, seeking the promise of warmth and beauty to come. It is only now, in middle age, that I begin to understand that winter is to be appreciated for itself. This is not an easy gratitude, yet it feels even deeper than the spontaneous sort that cascades from happy hearts.

Winter is not simply a passage between autumn glory and spring bounty. It is not only fallow. Indeed, winter is not empty at all. As gardeners are fully aware, it is a time of rest and renewal, of slow and slumbering growth. It is a time for regrouping, consolidating, gathering strength.

Winter has another face, one we usually think of as less benevolent, if no less "natural." Winter is a time for weeding out the weak plants, or those not adapted to our climate. Where a hundred infant lilies passed peacefully into autumn sleep, maybe only thirty will awake. Frost and root rots thin not only seedlings but mature plants that have passed their prime as well.

When a precious plant fails to reappear in spring, nature's relentless purging feels dreadfully sad. Indeed, I have sometimes replanted a pet five or six times, unwilling to accept that I can't grow absolutely everything I want to. Unwilling, too, to find an acceptable substitute in some of the many thousands of plants I can grow with relative ease.

When winter robs me of a beloved dream, I feel bitter against it, and start talking about moving to Eugene, or even California (Northern California, of course). If I can't get what I want here, then maybe I'll go where this bleakness doesn't happen. There are greener pastures, you know.

After I calm down (or visit California), I remember why I am here. Here, though outwardly quiet, winter is actually a time of enormous activity. If little is visible on the surface, a great deal is going on underground. Roots are lengthening. Pale shoots are inching upward through frozen soil, forcing their way up toward light and air. Embryo flowers are forming, their cramped folds tucked inside tightly compressed buds.

This implicit burgeoning has a powerful symbolic resonance because it echoes our own patterns of change. We, too, go through such periods. Life may seem drab and slack, empty and blank, yet under the skin we may be full almost to bursting with hidden riches. That very fullness creates a pressure that can be experienced as pain. Indeed, in medical terms pain *is* pressure.

Emotional pressure can hurt as much as any physical sensation. The building urgency of impending change, as experience is slowly pushing wisdom toward birth, can cause acute discomfort. I have no idea how a plant perceives winter, but for people there is comfort in recognizing these times of slow, sometimes painful growth for what they are.

When we don't see, until that newborn wisdom breaks the surface of our awareness, like a stubborn daffodil puncturing pavement, it can feel as though nothing at all is happening. Because our culture prizes the obvious, we experience our inner winter as empty waiting, frustrating and without fulfillment.

When only the pain is recognized, we struggle against the process. It helps to understand that hidden changes are occurring. When we can calm down and cooperate, breathing into the stillness, we can listen and learn a lot faster. Blooming spring can't come until solemn winter has prepared the way.

Hidden winter activity in the garden

This year, I am celebrating winter for itself. For the first time, I am seeing the sleeping garden as half full *and* half empty. I am thinking about the way those forced bulbs never really recover. A hyacinth that blooms indoors in January is truly spent. One that spends the winter building roots and rises to bloom in March or April will divide itself in a few years, splitting into several young bulbs. Now that is really something to celebrate.

Delightful Dogwoods
for Dark Days

 January

The damage wrought by our memorable wind and ice storms can leave gardeners all over the region wondering what to do. The answer is to do nothing. At least, nothing much. It's fine to remove huge branches from the garden (or your roof or the car), for example, and it's an excellent idea to repair broken water pipes or remove shattered pots from the garden. However, unless something really *needs* doing to the garden itself or the plants huddled in it, it's best, in the aftermath of a serious storm, to do nothing at all.

For one thing, when the ground is thoroughly wet, our very footsteps can harm plants that are just trying to get their sleep, thank you very much. Soggy footprints make for compacted soil, and may drown plant roots that are struggling to survive. What's more, the litter of broken branches left by big winds can successfully hide emergent plants that will not enjoy being trampled on by anybody's winter boots. If you can't clearly see where you are going, it's better not to go anywhere.

Really, after extreme rain or snow, the best thing we can do for our battered borders is stay out of them. If you need to get into a bed to remove branches, lay down a wide board first. Walk on that, and it will distribute your weight more evenly over a larger surface. Even small, relatively light people will adversely impact soil: When you stand on one foot (as we do, however briefly, when walking), that puts your full weight on a very small space. A hundred pounds spread over the surface area of a size four shoe sole creates a lot of pressure.

This is true even when the soil is fairly dry, but the problem is far worse in the rainy season. Wet soil compresses more than dry soil, and the damage lasts longer as well. Until the soil is fluffed up and the air can get back in, our plants will have a hard time breathing. Usually, worms do the fluffing for us. When worms are dormant or drowned, the soil can't be repaired except by hand. However, remedial soil work performed when the soil is wet will only make matters worse.

Our best bet, when faced with major storm damage, is to deal with the obvious, the dangerous, and the heartbreaking, as when large logs lie across your new *Cornus controversa* 'Variegata'. Even though you know you are simply making it easier for the deer to feast on the poor thing, do, by all means, set it free. But when you are done with that short list, just go back inside and try to forget the mess out there. To keep your mind occupied, turn your attention to the plant catalogs that are fast accumulating in that fireside basket. Console yourself by making a wish list of new and wonderful plants you'd like to be growing.

Most years, I try to keep that list small, because there's never enough room in the garden for all the newcomers. Stormy winters, however, almost guarantee that there'll be plenty of room. After the kind of relentless soaking that El Niño winters bring to our gardens, there will definitely be some losses. It's impossible not to mourn their passing. (Why is it that plants we feel ambivalent about are so very indestructible, while those we adore die with great goodwill?) It helps, however, to think of all the open slots they leave behind.

What better way to mark a new year in the garden than with a

What to do in the garden after winter storms

Red-stemmed dogwoods

Blood-twig dogwoods

celebratory nursery spree? The main point of this trip is renewal. Though the winter garden is less than prepossessing in a stormy year, it need not be utterly without charm or diversion. Winter shopping has the advantage of instantly improving the winter garden, since anything that catches your eye in January must have considerable winter presence. That goes double in a hard winter.

After a set of highly effective serial storms, I had quite a lot of opportunity for rethinking plant placement in my very young garden. The house wall plantings of mahonia and evergreen *Iris foetidissima* had been threaded with clumps of sweet-smelling *Sarcococca hookeriana* var. *humilis* which did not fare well under that deep blanket of snow, nor were they refreshed by the sweet rains — perhaps five inches in ten minutes was too much for them? We will never know, for they can no longer tell us. In any case, even before their passing, I had been wanting to replace some of them with a more striking winter accent shrub to place against the white house walls. (Maybe they sensed this lack of total approval, and hurt feelings hastened their departure.)

In any case, red-stemmed dogwoods had been suggested, and I was leaning toward a handsome Siberian with yellow-edged foliage called *Cornus alba* 'Spaethii'. These bushy, six-to-nine-foot shrubs have glowing red stems in winter, and make an attractive backdrop for a perennial or mixed border. As it happened, a midwinter nursery visit changed my mind instantly. I came home instead with several large plants of blood-twig dogwood, *Cornus sanguinea* 'Midwinter Fire'. This is an airy, open shrub with astonishingly lovely stems. In fall, as the leaves drop, they look softly golden. As the cold arrives, the stems heat up, changing color almost weekly.

The color intensifies steadily as winter progresses, so that by January, the 'Midwinter Fire' dogwoods appear to glow with an inner light. At their shrubby core, the branches are a luminous orange that builds to salmon, peach, and coral as the stems extend. Their tips are a sizzling combination of hot pinks and reds that do indeed decorate the house walls with flair and drama.

I had been tempted by a similar form called *C. s.* 'Winter Beauty', a handsome creature whose golden core builds slowly to sizzling reds at twigtip. These are sold as bare-root bundles, available exclusively from the Wayside Gardens catalog for $24.95. My 'Midwinter Fire' seemed like a better deal, at $19.95 for a five-gallon pot. Those I brought home (I definitely need a bigger car) were well-grown plants already four feet tall.

I picked my twiggy dogwoods up at my local nursery, Bay Hay and Feed on Bainbridge Island, in whose nursery I often console myself for the dear departed. It's also terrific for family visits, because there are plenty of things to entertain the nongardeners while we greenies are busy browsing. Clothing, tools, and all kinds of useful gadgets lure guys in to the main store. Kids gravitate toward the model farm machinery, fake frogs, and terrific pet toys. Fred and Ethel, Bay Hay's pet turkeys, are joined in season by boxes of cheeping chicks and baby bunnies as well.

> RESOURCES
>
> BAY HAY AND FEED NURSERY
> 10355 NE VALLEY ROAD
> BAINBRIDGE ISLAND, WA
> 206/842-5274
>
> WAYSIDE GARDENS
> 1 GARDEN LANE
> HODGES, SC 29695-0001
> 800/845-1124

Nurseries like this are well worth seeking out, because family trips can brighten those interminable days when the skies seem determined to empty themselves on our gardens. When the play-dough has dried out, the kids have already seen all the videos, and Mom just can't face reading Tin Tin out loud and doing all the voices *right,* it's time for a nursery break. Even if you don't bring anything home, visiting plants renews the communal spirit that enforced indoor time can diminish. And if you should happen to find just the right pot of jasmine to bring home, remember that it's a gift for the whole family, for everybody will be cheered by its willing blossoms, spilling their sweetness while the rain comes down.

Most regional nurseries are well supplied in the gray days, not just with twiggy dogwoods, but with winter-blooming viburnums, budded witch hazels, and flowering camellias. If you decide to treat your garden to one or two of these charmers, plunk them in orna-mental pots until the ground is ready to work, and delight in their refreshing presence. Let's ring in the new year with jubilation, gar-nishing our sodden gardens as we gladden our sore hearts.

Gardening from Scratch

January

Several years ago, I had to leave my maturing island garden
and strike out for new territory. The first year was one of
tremendous transition — it was enough just to find my feet as
a single parent. However, I desperately missed the daily act
of gardening. Since my rental place did not permit garden
making, various friends offered me the use of their weeds.
Eventually a gardenless friend called with a proposal: If he
rented a newly built woodland cottage, would I make a
garden for it? When I arrived to look it over, the owners
offered to help pay for improvements and reduce the rent as
well. Such inducements offset the inconvenience of gardening away from home, so I spent that winter planning and
plotting and in April of 1996, we began the joyful process of
gardening from scratch.

This was literally true, for the site had been scraped to
hardpan during construction. Not a blade of grass was left,
and the ragged edge of the woods, which encircled the house
to the north and east, was considerably higher than the
remaining soil level. To rectify this, we made gentle berms
that brought the garden beds up to the level of the woods
and left the paths lower. The first paths encircled the house
in lapping curves. They were laid down with weed cloth,

then graveled to a depth of about five inches. I started planting on the north side of the house, where the bare new paths were edged with golden *Hakonechloa macra* 'Aureola' and black mondo grass (*Ophiopogon planiscapens* 'Nigrescens'), as well as white wood aster (*Aster divaricatus*) and a number of subtly patterned heucheras like 'Eco Magnificent' and 'Greenfinch', all of which thrive in damp shade.

In the beds behind the paths, native plants like sword ferns, huckleberry, madronas, and salal were edited rather than removed. Mossy stumps and nurse logs were left in place and only lightly tidied up. To make the transition between woods and garden as visually convincing as possible, we used open, fine-textured shrubs like azaleas and many kinds of dogwoods, including good forms of our native *Cornus nuttallii* ('Colrigo Giant' and the hybrid 'Eddie's White Wonder') and *C. stolonifera*, including red, green, and golden twigged forms. These were supplemented with bold-leaved perennials, including numerous ligularias, rodgersias, and hostas as well as native veratrums, boykinias, and *Darmera peltata*.

Acid and gritty, the subsoil in the open part of the garden was virtually sterile, and it took months of amendment with compost and manure before we saw the first worms. Since both winter and spring were wet, we didn't realize until midsummer that small, hidden seeps were keeping the borders saturated in several areas, both sunny and shady. When we dug down to look at the roots of some obviously struggling plants, we discovered that they were sitting in half a foot of water, despite being on a fairly steep slope. This lost us some trees and shrubs, including a pink-berried *Sorbus hupehensis* and a previously lusty *Aralia chinensis*, but by raising bed levels and using more water-tolerant plants, we managed to replant these places successfully. Purple hazel (*Corylus maxima* 'Purpurea'), a dainty 'Red Jade' crab apple, several willows, and *Nyssa sylvatica* are doing well there now, underplanted with a host of perennial swamp mallows (*Euphorbia palustris*), and swamp sunflower (*Helianthus angustifolius*).

Planning
a garden
in winter

Half sloping, sunny meadow, half shady woods' edge, part wet clay and part dry, sandy soil, this garden offers ample opportunities for growing a wide range of plants. The shady places made homes for many of the plants rescued from the old garden and held for me by kind friends, who added plenty of others from their own gardens when it came time to reclaim them. An enormous quantity of splendid trees and shrubs came from two generous nursery owners, Peter Ray of Puget Garden Resources and John Kimble of Green Arrow Nursery, both of Vashon Island. These gift plants were invaluable, for many of them were large enough to have an immediate impact on the landscape. The bulk of the trees and large shrubs formed the spine of a long mixed border that screens the garden from the next cottage. In several places, thickets of lacecap hydrangeas and Asian leatherleaf (*Mahonia bealei*) interweave with native huckleberries and salal to make visual baffles and practical barriers. (There are quite a few dogs and children in the neighborhood.)

It is not always a delight to work with plants not of one's own choosing, but I was very lucky in this respect. Peter Ray donated dozens of wonderful dogwoods, both shrubs and trees, including several or many of each variety, as well as masses of choice hydrangeas and a goodly selection of mahonias. As an ardent collector, I tend to favor variety over those desirable sweeps we urge one another to create. Through Pete's generosity, my new garden has both, and the result is beautiful as well as satisfying to the spirit.

John Kimble, a horticulturist with the Seattle Parks Department, was in the process of closing down his small private nursery, finding that two full-time jobs were too much. He brought me the pick of the leftovers, many of them plants from his personal collection. A few, like a gigantic katsura and a magnificent old *Euonymus europaeus*, had been in pots for years. The huge rootballs required a strong-backed crew to move and transplant, but these large plants gave the infant garden an instant impression of maturity.

Smaller trees have become centerpieces for various sections of the deep borders that embrace the cottage. Dainty *Stewartia monadelpha* nestles between *Hypericum androsaemum* 'Albury Purple' and

Callicarpa bodinieri 'Profusion', their lower reaches threaded with *Alstroemeria psittacina* 'Variegata', whose rich red and green flowers glow against the stewartia's autumn foliage. Clumps of blood grass (*Imperata cylindrica* 'Rubra') add to the fire, which is damped down by swirls of lacy black chervil (*Anthriscus sylvestris* 'Ravenswing') and the chartreuse wands of *Euphorbia schillingii*.

In another corner, *Styrax obassia* dangles clusters of pallid flowers over thickets of white masterwort (*Astrantia major*) and blue balloon flowers (*Platycodon grandiflorus*). The foliage of these turns a clear, singing gold in fall, when the stems keel over to reveal a swath of purple *Colchicum autumnale* in full bloom. The pale orange styrax bark shimmers like Thai silk when wet with winter rain, echoed by spiky, upright *Carex buchananii* 'Red Racer' and red-twigged dogwood, *Cornus alba* 'Sibirica'. Several witch hazels, including my beloved and intensely fragrant *Hamamelis mollis* 'Pallida', form a small stand, thickly interplanted with winter blooming laurel spurge (*Daphne laureola*), also strongly scented. A pair of standard × *Sycoparrotia semidecidua* is guarded by a shaggy lion's head maple and a flock of dark-flowered *Helleborus orientalis*.

The back side of the cottage holds deep, sunny borders full of hundreds of compact border shrubs woven with perennials, while the small deck is laced with vines and climbers. Already, there are far too many plants to mention (or count). Thanks to abundant quantities of manure and compost, they flourished so well that by the end of the first summer, the beds were sumptuously overflowing. As autumn slid away, the wisdom of planning a garden in winter became clear. Everywhere, evergreens linked with handsome deciduous trees and shrubs to define and shape the garden. If summer was past and autumn nearly spent, the garden was still full of flowers and buds that promised life and color for many months to come. When we give that quietest of seasons its due, the garden remains furnished in all times and weathers.

Hardy Plants

January

Magazines and newspapers are full of articles discussing
the long-term weather trends, collectively known as El
Niño (the warming trend) and La Niña (the cooling trend).
Gardeners don't need a lot of scientists to explain what is
perfectly obvious to those of us who struggle to have something in bloom (or at least looking decent) all year long.
Winter gardeners are all too aware that plants that will succeed with panache in a mild winter can look like hammered—let's say manure—in a harsh one.

The result is that many Northwestern gardeners are mod-
ifying their palettes, choosing rock-hardy plants for high-
performance positions and relegating the half-hardies to less
obtrusive spots. They do this not in despair, but realizing
patiently that within a few years, perhaps a decade, the
trends will once again reverse. Experienced gardeners are
well aware of these periodic weather cycles, which have
been occurring since time out of mind.

What amuses the older folks is the periodic recurrence of
brash young gardeners who think they have discovered borderline hardy plants. Why isn't everybody growing every
jasmine, these hotheads demand to know. What's wrong with
these people that they don't pack their yards with plumbago?

Where are all the New Zealand plants we could be growing? Why stick with the boring old favorites?

Well, there is something to be said for such queries, and I have made more than a few of them myself. Botanists and plant scientists say that we in the maritime Northwest enjoy a modified Mediterranean climate. That means I can grow anything Mediterranean, right? After many enthusiastic plungings into the Mediterranean flora, I've learned that we can indeed grow lots of Mediterranean, from shrubby herbs like rosemary, lavender, sage, and thyme to perennials like *Euphorbia characias* and the treelike *E. mellifera*. Well, maybe not. Those scientists are right in one sense—we have wet winters and dry summers. However, we don't have the heat that plants learned to appreciate in, say, southern Italy. Without it, they can't always be convinced to stick around very long. And that honey-bush spurge, *E. mellifera*? Try zone 10. Yes, it made it through a few winters. However, it usually looked like something the cat was too proud to drag in. When I heard myself defending it to another, less besotted gardener, saying, "Give it time to come around; it's only August," I realized that I loved the idea of the plant more than the plant itself. The fact is, we *do* have a modified Mediterranean climate. The modifications are (1) no sun, and (2) constant rain. Small points, perhaps, but they add up.

Borderline hardy plants

Tassel bush

Sir Charles Lemon rhododendron

R. williamsianum

Other of my plant experiments came about because of Elizabeth Lawrence, a garden writer from North Carolina. When I discovered a battered old copy (since reprinted, I'm glad to say) of her book *A Southern Garden*, her writing made me determined to grow everything she wrote about. After all, according to the USDA zone map, both Raleigh and Seattle are zone 8. We ought to be able to do whatever they can, right?

Not really. The South enjoys far more accumulated heat than we do, and gets hot summer nights, where ours tend to cool off quickly. They can ripen wood and seed on plants that never quite mature here in the Northwest. They also have more summer humidity, on average, than we do. (Recent summers may make this statement questionable, but if we view weather trends over a longer haul—say, ten or twenty years—our summers are decidedly dry.) Anyway, suffice it to say that as I grew my way through Elizabeth Lawrence's book, the failures outnumbered the successes. Indeed, she herself often remarked that this or that plant was really not worth growing, since it recovered so slowly after a bad winter. It just took me a little longer to hear that part.

At first, I jumped into my plant trials with both feet. My Seattle porch was draped not just with hardy *Akebia quinata*, whose purple flowers smelled so chocolaty in late winter, but with jasmines, which I replaced every few years. (I have since learned this is called "zonal denial," a term coined by Sean Hogan when he moved from the Bay Area to Portland.) I also grew something I had fallen for when reading an article about a garden in Wales: *Lapageria rosea*, the national flower of Chile. I persuaded a friend working in Chile to find and send me seeds, which I excitedly grew in the dim basement fastnesses where most of my Seattle garden first saw light.

In those days, it was a challenge to find uncommon perennials, so I grew nearly all of my own, relying on seed exchanges and international catalogs. Rare vines were especially scarce, and I had fun growing lots of species clematis from seed. The *Lapageria* sprouted nicely, and I got half a dozen sturdy little plants. I set them out with care in favored spots all over the yard, where they faded away one by one. Most went down under determined slug onslaughts. (Why do slugs have such extraordinary tastes? They also ate a whole brugmansia I grew from that same seed batch—and those are so hallucinogenic as to be incredibly toxic, but that's another story.) Of the rest, the cats toasted one, I'm pretty sure, while embracing to death the pink and cream *Actinidia kolomikta* at its side. The last one, wrapped in the arms of another Chilean climber, the orange daisy-flowered *Mutisia clematis*, froze during a hard winter. So, of course, did the mutisia. Oh well.

My gardenias—surely they will love that southern corner!—

suffered similar fates, as did scores of other must-have plants that
somebody—anybody—had claimed were hardy here. In those days,
I took such losses very hard. Indeed, after the blasting winter of
1990, removing all those frozen eucryphias made me cry. A whole
bunch of garden friends got together that year and had a group
whine about our favorite dead (we each got five minutes to mourn).
The upshot, however, was quite positive. Each of us also had to
come up with a list of surprises: plants that had amazed us by
coming through that difficult stretch with aplomb. These became
stock plants for friends and nurseries. From them, a whole batch of
hardier plants came forth. *Ceanothus thyrsiflorus* 'Victoria', a genuinely tough little shrub, got its recognition that year. Hardy rose-
maries, sages, and lavenders were tracked down and propagated.
Hardy herbs were used to refurbish depleted nursery stocks, along
with many other survivors.

That kind of response—mourning followed by restorative
action—made us feel better and made our gardens look lastingly
better. I and many others like me got tired of having the most expensive compost in town. Yes, it's fun to be a front-runner, showing the
way to others. However, frontline gardening can leave your borders
looking like a reenactment of wagon train days, when the narrow
trails over the steepest mountain passes were strewn with the dead.
Historical garden restoration is all very well in its place, but some
scenes, and even whole periods, are best left veiled by the kindly
curtain of time.

If we look to our invaluable elders for guidance, seeing which
plants adventurous longtime gardeners plan their own garden designs
around, we often find that they have quietly been growing a host of
utterly hardy treasures for donkey's years. At Nan Ballard's garden
in Issaquah, Washington, we find the original *Garrya* × *issaquahensis*
(a natural hybrid between our native *G. elliptica* and the California
G. fremontii), which was recognized and introduced to the trade by
Nan's sister, who is commemorated in the finest form, 'Pat Ballard'.
This handsome native evergreen is called tassel bush for the
long, dangling catkins, which can be six or seven inches long in

a good form. Even after a grisly winter, it looks tidy and well furnished, unlike many borderline hardy evergreens, which often look worse than frankly deciduous things after severe cold.

The presence of our native rhododendrons makes it seem natural to introduce Asian species as well, many of which look comfortably at home in woodsy, shaded gardens. Though innumerable species and hybrids are famously happy here, those with huge, tropical-looking leaves often get hammered by frost. That leaves us with only about ten thousand others to chose amongst, not all of which have equal charms. In the long run, it's worth selecting rhododendrons for their year-round good looks, rather than simply for their flowers. The best offer good form, extraordinary presence, and the air of distinction that nature confers upon her own favorites in any category.

At Eulalie Wagner's garden in Lakewold, near Tacoma, a mature Sir Charles Lemon rhododendron rises a good twenty-five feet above the entry drive, displaying its arboreal nature most impressively. This choice shrub (or, eventually, tree) offers us not only distinguished form but lovely foliage, long and felted and backed with velvety cinnamon-colored indumentum, which reflects the evening sun in winter with the rosy luster of alpenglow. Its flowers are similarly luminous, arriving in great trusses of fluted trumpets the gelid yellow of lemon sorbet and with a tangy, lemony scent. If you don't have room for a tree, try your hand at the choicest of the remainder, browsing through pygmy forms to garden queens. Maybelle Johnson, also of Issaquah, gave me a shimmering little R. *williamsianum* from her old garden, which I treasure. Compact and beautifully formed, its glossy, bronze-tinted leaves are trimmed in season with plump trusses of palest pink bells, neatly freckled with rose. Always a modest grower, it can be held in a large container for years, if need be. The new host of little yaks (offspring of the silvery leaved R. *yakushimanum*) are small enough for the tiniest garden. Though rhododendrons have long been out of high horticultural fashion (except, of course, for those ultra-tender Vireyas), many species are gloriously good looking in any season and are well worth seeking out at specialist's nurseries. After trying times have left younger gardens looking sorry, a timely visit to older gardens will reveal an extensive catalog of excellent, reliable species to start with.

In Seattle's Highlands, Betty Miller left a legacy of a garden, full of rare plants of every description. The backbone of her garden, however, was built upon utterly hardy evergreens, including a number of uncommon conifers. Most memorable among them, to me, was a weeping Atlas cedar. Icy blue and dripping with icicle pale branches, potently sculptural in form, it came through the hardest winter unscathed.

This is not to say that we should not try new things. All of these fine gardeners were well known for trying new things and would be the last ones to discourage active experimentation in the next generation. However, each of them has told me some variation of what Betty Miller expressed so well: "Fancy plants are the icing in the garden. If your important plants are solidly hardy, it won't be so painfully obvious that you've made a fool of yourself over some tender rarity. Of course, you'll go out and do it again with something else—we all do. That's the fun of it, isn't it?"

FEBRUARY

Preserving Pussywillows

 February

For many years, my children collected bouquets of catkins for my youngest son's birthday in mid-January. Silky gray and soft as kittens, these fat, furry flowers came from an elderly scouler willow (*Salix scouleriana*) in our front yard. The year we moved from the farm, we had to wander farther afield to glean our twigs, but it didn't take more than a few minutes of driving to locate a good-sized pussy willow blooming away by the roadside. Though this native species is rarely grown in gardens, it is a highly ornamental creature, with dappled bark; sinuous, often multiple trunks; and lightly felted, silver-backed leaves. Mature specimens are invaluable in the garden, where they make a handsome backdrop or centerpiece for a mixed border.

In the wild, scouler willows grow into graceful small trees (fifteen to thirty feet), but in small gardens they are easily kept shrubby by regular thinning. If a young plant is cut back when planted, it will develop into a multiple-trunked shrub about the size of a mature lilac bush. The largest of the trunks can be removed every few years to maintain this compact size. Where room permits, one or two main trunks can be encouraged and the lower branches trimmed up to create a pleasantly shaped little tree.

Like many willows, scouler willow trees are rather brittle of branch, blithely shedding heavy older limbs with every windstorm. Shrubbier scoulers don't have this habit, which becomes a distinct liability when they are underplanted with perennials. Cutting them back in youth may seem harsh, but it makes them better behaved — and thus more lastingly welcome — in mixed company.

Even mature trees can be cut back quite hard, as we discovered at the farm. The last several years we spent there were windy ones, and great chunks of this tree came down each winter, with occasional drop-ins in summer as well. They would invariably land on top of their most fragile neighbors, flattening many a promising peony and rose in full bud. The last such event was so infuriating that it reminded me of a sage old saying about the best defense. Out came the handsaw and down came the last remaining major limbs. (I think that an elderly tree deserves to go down through hand-to-hand combat, rather than fall to the casual impersonality of a chain saw. After all, it took that tree years to grow so large. It's only fitting that it should cost us some time and effort to cut it down.)

Had that tree retained its lovely natural shape, such powerful offensive action might not have seemed a good idea. However, frequent loss of limb had left our scouler willow less than lovely, so this radical pruning did no harm. In fact, a number of lusty side shoots were already heading heavenward. In an amazingly short time, the tree was rejuvenated, with healthy, shapely young branches replacing the rotting old ones.

Very few nurseries carry scouler willows, but anybody who so desires can have as many as they like for the price of a drive in the country. Scouler willow is common along Washington roadsides (indeed, it grows all the way from Alaska to New Mexico). Keep your eye out for the upright, shrubby plants that often decorate the verges of country roads. (Young scoulers cut back by road-clearing crews respond with lush growth that results in dense shrubs rather than airy trees.) In February and March, scoulers are very obvious, for nearly every twig is tipped with large and lustrous pussies. Indeed, I can't understand why scouler willows aren't common in gardens, for their pussies are larger and more beautiful than the horticultural pussywillows widely sold in nurseries and garden centers. What's more, scouler pussies appear a good deal earlier than their foreign counterparts. Since most pussy willows are grown entirely for the beauty of their silky catkins, it seems curious to neglect this splendid native in favor of frumpier plants with fewer charms.

When you find a likely-looking candidate, whip out your pruning snips and thoughtfully relieve the tree of some of its excess twiggery. When cutting pussy willows for the house, we naturally want to take the most heavily decorated twigs. For propagation purposes, however, it's good to include a few bits of green wood as well. Small branches that are prime for rooting are described in horticultural terms as feeling firm rather than "lishy." Such twigs are not rigid: They have a bit of give to them, yet aren't so soft as to be swished about like ribbons. Actually, willows root with such alacrity that practically any piece will take. Indeed, willow water—water in which a bundle of freshly cut twigs has been steeped—was the original rooting hormone. To get cuttings to root quickly, water them in with willow water and watch them take off. In most woody plants, mature wood is usually difficult or impossible to root, yet some years back we stuck a dozen willow limbs as big as my arm (shed during a windstorm) straight into the ground, and every one of them set roots and grew.

Early catkins

Scouler
willows

Rooting extract

When you get your bounty home, just stick your willow twigs into a jar of water. Keep them on a sunny windowsill, and in a few weeks you will discover many long, white roots. Plants rooted in water often need a bit of transition before placement in dirt, but not willows. Pot them up if you aren't sure where you want them; otherwise you can set the young plants wherever you like in the garden. Keep them moist for the first summer, but once they are

RESOURCES

FORESTFARM
990 TETHEROW ROAD
WILLIAMS, OR 97544

established, scouler willows thrive in good soils, even without sup-
plemental water. If you can't find any good-looking willows locally,
consult the Forestfarm catalog for a large selection of native and
other fascinating willows. Either way, home grown or imported,
next year, you will be admiring the year's first catkins without leaving home.

Growing Cat Food

February

One fall, a review copy of a new garden book arrived on my doorstep in a huge box. Besides the book (a really fun one called *Women of Flowers*), the box also held a thriving cymbidium orchid in full flower. Though I don't usually grow them, I love the exotic look of orchids. I set this sunny little creature right by the kitchen sink, where I could admire it daily. Soon, however, it started to look a bit shaggy. Those long, lush leaves grew tattered and torn.

The problem was clearly not a disease. This kind of damage is caused only by physical force of some kind. It might have taken longer to figure out what was happening, except for one tip-off. A pot of miniature daffodils on the windowsill nearby had similar leaf damage, and all the new buds were bitten clean off.

Now, no slug or creepy-crawly does that. Deer, yes, but I was quite certain that no deer had been in the kitchen. There were, however, two active young kittens, curious and full of bounce. Indeed, their depredations had already limited the size and kind of plants I could grow indoors. There was only one place in the house they couldn't reach yet—an upper shelf on my office bookcase. Because it is not very near a window, plants grown there became lanky quite quickly. My solution was to bring home those delicious pots of bulbous iris and hyacinths, enjoy them until they flopped, then move them outside into the garden.

This worked very nicely for the bulbs, but I would have liked to enjoy those bright blossoms a little longer. The orchid affair made me crabby enough to consider a new tactic. First, I consulted with my cats' favorite vet, Elizabeth Greenlees-Cooper, who has a home-visit practice.

The last time I had called Liz, it was because the pupil of my cat's eye was the size of the full moon. Not both, mind you. Just one. Back when I worked as a nurse, I saw a lot of brain damage, and this huge, staring pupil looked like bad news.

In a human, having one eye completely dilated and unresponsive to light would suggest brain trauma or a tumor. Because this condition happened in a matter of minutes, I thought both ideas improbable. Liz and her partner, Julia Atwood, arrived in their Roadrunner Vet Van and agreed. Liz then decided it looked like a case of atropine poisoning, which made me think about the plants I was growing indoors. Among them were some brugmansias (formerly classed as *Daturas*). As I have often mentioned, these South American plants are dazzlers, with huge, fluted flowers and giant tropical leaves. They are also extremely potent psychotropic drug plants, used shamanistically for millennia. Used right, these plants allow you to see heaven and come home to tell about it. Used wrong, they're a one-way ticket.

My little Lily had been fooling around behind the potted plants. Sure enough, we found a freshly broken stem near floor level. Half of Lily was seeing heaven and the other half was seeing a Bainbridge Island ranch house. No wonder the poor girl was acting weird.

Since Liz proved to be so clever about drug-abusing cats, I thought she would offer sage advice about cat food, and I was right. This time, Liz looked at the orchid, then looked at the cats, and said the little darlings were indeed the culprits but not to be cross with them. They needed, she explained, something fresh and green to eat. Cat salad? Well, not exactly. However, grass of several kinds is a valuable aid to kitty digestion. Cats that don't get outside to graze on the lawn often benefit from a pot or two of wheat grass or oat grass, two especial favorites.

I then called the local nurseries, seeking cat-friendly plants. Several years ago, I recalled seeing ads for sturdy indoor planters full of good things for cats to chew on. Now, however, the fad seemed to have passed and the pickings were slimmer. In nearby Rolling Bay, Bay Hay and Feed Nursery had a cute little container with a smiling kitty face bristling with stick-out whiskers. Open it, dump in the enclosed packet of vermiculite, sprinkle on the enclosed seeds, and voila! Instant cat food.

The package—which is called OzzyAtt The Incredible Edible Radical Cat, and cost about $5—was a huge hit with my kids. The cats were also impressed, at least at first. The advertised "herbal hair" (really just wheat grass) appeared in a few days. As the first shoots elongated, the kittens happily dragged quite a lot of the seedlings out of the lightweight medium, leaving them daintily draped over the countertop.

As the grass rooted in better and grew more vigorously, the cats nibbled the ends. Sometimes I even caught them playing with the grassy shoots. They would lie on their backs in the sun, batting away at the green strands and purring vigorously. Great! It really works!

Friendly cats and cat-friendly plants

However, given the choice, the cats still prefer houseplants. I know this because, encouraged by their grass-snacking, I went out and bought more indoor plants. A large, rosy azalea in a pretty pot. A group of scented mini-daffodils. A pink-budded jasmine bursting out of its container.

I figured that, given their initial interest in the wheat grass, which is supposedly healthier and better for them, they would leave my new plants alone. Ha! The azalea, it's true, they did not eat. This is good, because some azaleas (and rhododendrons) are toxic to animals and humans.

No, my darling kittens did not eat the rosy azalea in its pretty pot. The little brats merely tossed it off the refrigerator and watched it explode all over the kitchen floor. They then ran off giggling, presumably seeking greener pastures for their mischief. Bad kitty! After I cleaned that mess up, I discovered that they had again bitten all the buds off the daffodils and had started on the jasmine. The daffodils went straight outside, where they will rebloom in peace next year. The jasmine got repotted into a large hanging basket with a drip-free bottom. This is now hanging in the bathroom, where it gets plenty of indirect light and all the ambient moisture it desires. Without anybody chewing on it, it blooms like crazy, especially when I remember to feed it on a regular basis.

And the cats? Well, I decided to keep the experiment going. I bought an ounce each of wheat grass and oat grass seed and sowed several larger potsful. The trick to getting the cats to use these pots, rather than grazing on my houseplants, seems to be a combination of several things.

First, keep one grass pot in the same place all the time, preferably next to the water bowl. (Actually, my cats drink out of a flower vase, but that's another story . . .)

Second, keep the grass coming. Fresh grass seems more interesting than elderly grass.

Third, each time you introduce a new plant into the house, set a pot of young grass (we're still talking wheat or oats here) next to the newcomer.

Fourth, be ready to try lots of plants until you find ones the cats don't eat.

Fifth, look for plants cats *do* eat that are not bad for them. A reader who has been a horticulturist for her whole life passed on a hot tip: Cats love spider plants (*Chlorophytum comosum*), which, heaven knows, are the comeback kings of the plant world. Chew their tops off and presto, these willing lily relatives will produce five new babies, shooting them out on aerial stems to replace the bitten one.

This may sound like too much trouble, but think of it this way: The research will involve buying and trying all kinds of new plants. A tough job, as we have often noted before, but hey, somebody's got to do it.

Hand in Glove

 February

This winter, I've been putting in a new garden, which means doing my share of mucking about in the chilly mud. The only remarkable thing about this is that this is the first winter I can recall when I haven't had horribly chapped hands. The reason is simple: Finally I've found a garden glove I can actually wear.

Gardeners seem to come in two categories—those who wear gloves and those who buy gloves and don't wear them. Most of the nonwearers *want* to wear gloves. Indeed, our often impressive glove collections are mute testimony to our willingness to be convinced. The problem is the gloves themselves. Most of them just aren't comfortable for long. They make your hands too sweaty or don't provide enough protection from weather or nettles or rose thorns. Often their seams bite us when we perform repeated movements like pruning. Some are okay for some things. The inexpensive gloves sold for dishwashing are great for handling shredded bark. They do have a few drawbacks, though: They tear readily, fit badly, and smell absolutely revolting after a few uses.

Many men don't get what the issue is. They seem content with almost any big work gloves, but women are less well served. Work gloves rarely fit small hands well, and kids' garden gloves that do fit aren't made to stand up to prolonged use. The real difficulty, however, is that most glove materials don't allow for enough feeling. Even those of us who enjoy physical contact with our plants tend to wear gloves when it's cold and wet out there. At least, we try to wear them, but two minutes after we hunker down for some quiet dividing or seed planting, we strip those gloves off in frustration. What's so great about having dry hands if you can't *do* anything with them?

Now, however, I find myself wearing a certain pair of garden gloves for hours at a stretch. They have enough grip that I can carry oversized, slippery rootballs or tumbling masses of crocosmia corms without dropping any. They remain comfortable when I'm shoveling or trundling a wheelbarrow. They keep my hands pleasantly warm and dry despite damp, chilly weather. They function especially nicely when I'm gathering seed, dividing smaller plants, and teasing apart fine roots. Such detail work is where many okay gloves fall down, but these don't muffle finger sensitivity or make my hands feel clumsy when working with tiny seeds. Best of all, they really fit my small hands.

I was introduced to them by Joe Piecuch, the head of the grounds and horticulture crews at the Bloedel Reserve. We often garden together, and I couldn't help but notice that he had about six pairs of glowing orange gloves in the back of his car. I also noticed how grumpy he became when the winsome dog next door playfully removed some of them for a quick game of catch. I further noticed that he didn't feel the penetrating cold of the wet, mucky soil we were digging in. He told me to try a pair, so I did, and though they were too big, it was immediately apparent that these gloves were thin enough to have great hand feel and yet provided great insulation for cold and damp. That day, I got a pair of my own and soon boasted half a dozen, all of which are in frequent use. (I like to change my gloves—and socks—a lot in wet weather.)

For many of you, the Ultimate Garden Gloves must not be news. The company's booth at a recent Northwest Flower and Garden Show was continually crowded with gardeners snapping up these sleek orange beauties. "People love the way they provide both great grip and real flexibility," explains Jennifer Kowalski, who distributes the gloves out of Rolling Bay, Washington. "They are also reasonably priced, at around $10 a pair, which also helps." Kowalski's sister-in-law, Melissa, started the business a few years ago with Jennifer's brother, Dan Kowalski. "My brother Dan had been using a similar glove for everything from carpentry to gutting fish," Jennifer recounts. "One day, Melissa's cotton garden gloves gave out as usual, so she grabbed Dan's. She loved them,

The Ultimate Garden Gloves

and as a Master Gardener, she knew a lot of other people would, too. They followed some leads and discovered how they could import these gloves. They're made in Malaysia, and they really fit smaller hands well, making them very popular with women."

Together, the Kowalskis set up the Ultimate Glove Company and watched it take off almost immediately. "The rubber is the perfect weight and give, thick enough to protect the skin, thin enough to allow real mobility. It's neat, because people who can't stand the inflexibility of gloves become total converts. Using these gloves is approaching cult status in some places," Jennifer Kowalski reports with a grin.

The only problem is that some of their distributors liked the gloves so much that they began importing them as well, using different names. "Welcome to free enterprise!" Kowalski says, adding, "Our first response was dismay, but we decided to develop more products with similar qualities. This time, though, we'll try to make them patentable!"

Despite the competition, Ultimate Gloves continue to sell well. "We have a lot of repeat customers who want to share them with friends," Kowalski says. "Our gloves are seamless, so they never rub you wrong. They can be laundered, and they dry very quickly. Most gardeners love the protective long cuff, but our Ultimate G-3 glove, which is green, has a shorter cuff for those who prefer that style."

Gardeners who find rubber gloves too sweaty will appreciate the Kowalskis' lightweight gloves. "The Ultimate Summer Glove is made of a fine but strong mesh weave that's highly breathable. Only the front of each glove is rubberized, so your hands don't overheat," she points out.

Like the winter version, these summer-weight gloves mimic the natural shape of the hand, making them very comfortable to wear. The gently curved fingers and palm cup your hand, and even confirmed nonwearers will be pleasantly surprised at their handling skills. Indeed, just for fun I tried typing this chapter in them. The fact that you can read this says a lot about their finesse!

In summer, rubber gloves of any kind can get first sweaty, then stinky. I rarely use gloves in summer, when the soil is warm, but those who do know that this allegation is indeed true. Fortunately, there are a number of good ways to avoid smelly gloves. First is to develop the habit of turning your gloves inside out. No, not while you are wearing them (though that might give you great traction), but each time you remove them. Usually, it's enough to pull the cuffs back about halfway, exposing the hand and finger parts to fresh air. This lets them ventilate and dry quickly, thus eliminating excess moisture and that distinctive smell, so reminiscent of an adolescent boy's sneakers.

Those with large hands may find it necessary to completely reverse the gloves, pulling the fingers inside out individually. If you find a glove with the right fit, you can often reverse gloves just by peeling them off quickly. Some do this with finesse by pulling backward slowly but steadily while keeping the material flat and close to the hand. Either way, if it works, you can air out your gloves easily. If the gloves are too tight, reversing them can be a fiddly business, especially for people with big fingers. Here, the solution is to trade chores with a neat-fingered person, swapping glove reversal for, say, boot removal. (Rubber boots can be even harder to take off than tight gloves.)

Some well-made rubber gloves, including the Ultimate Gloves, can be washed in the washing machine. Presoak revolting-smelling gloves in water with a few tablespoons of baking soda; this eliminates the stink factor in a hurry. However, I'm afraid that no washable rubber gloves can go in the dryer. They all need to be line-dried, preferably inside out.

This leads to the next piece of the solution: Have more. I commonly keep anywhere from three to six pairs of gloves around. Like socks, gloves are most pleasant to use when dry. If you have plenty of pairs, you can put on a fresh one each time you take a break. I also keep extra pairs in other sizes than my own, so that visiting friends can be coaxed into a companionable weeding session. Small ones come in handy for visiting kids or adults (like me) whose paws are undersized. It's also wise to have large gloves ready for the day when an oversized visitor offers to help out with those really big jobs.

In my garden, there are always heavy pots and small trees waiting to be moved. If you too have ambitious projects that are temporarily on hold for lack of muscle power, having extra gloves to offer can mean the difference between frustration and instant gratification. In terms of keeping gloves dry, there are as many ideas about how to do that as there are gardeners. Some people swear by talcum or baby powder, which they apply liberally to the inside of their gloves. One guy I know uses foot powder, but I don't even want to think about that. Anyway, talc is fine if you can keep your powder dry, but that only works in the westerns. In my experience, combining gloves and powder has always made a horrid paste that cakes to both my hands and the inside of the gloves. Since so many people have suggested this and insist that they actually do it themselves, I suspect my technique is simply poor.

However, I recently started using baking soda on summer-stinky gloves, figuring that if it could make my refrigerator smell clean, it could deodorize anything at all. I pour a teaspoon or so into each glove after use, then dump it out before putting them on the next time. This does indeed remove the wet-rubber odor, and it keeps my hands a little drier as well. If roses are anything to go by, it's probably actively preventing black spot and coral rust on my hands as well.

Several gardeners more stylish than I prefer a combination of gloves. These gals all start by smearing their hands with some kind of hand cream (Eucerin, a wax-based, nonscented cream get high praise from this crowd). Next, they slip on thin cotton liner gloves. Over those, they tug on the rubber gloves. Thus fortified, the ladies say they can face anything the garden throws at them and emerge with their perfect hands unscathed. More power to them, but I personally can't feel anything with so many layers between me and the soil or roots or whatever.

Besides, since my hands weren't perfect when they went into the gloves, I can't fairly expect them to look fabulous when they come out. At best, they look battered and slightly the worse for wear. After wearing rubber gloves, they look a little pruney but are far less filthy than usual about the nails. No, I'm not looking for Maidenform hands, just unscarred and relatively clean ones. Gloves that allow me to garden with grace while remaining fairly dry win my wholehearted approval. If they stink, well, my advice is to treat them like sneakers. Wash them often, air them well, and wear them in good health.

In Seattle, Ultimate Garden Gloves are available at Molbak's Nursery and City People's Nursery. For information on where you can purchase the gloves elsewhere, contact Jennifer Kowalski at 888/880-1997 (toll-free) or 206/842-8963. You can also visit their Web site (www.ultimategoods.com).

Flame On, Slug Breath!

 February

Whenever I write about techniques for weed control, one in particular seems to catch people's fancy. I receive multiple requests for more information on how flame-throwers can kill garden weeds. Still others want to know how to harness fire power to kill slugs. Finally, several people always offer warnings, describing how somebody (always somebody else) set the house/garage/barn on fire when "weeding" with a flamethrower.

Clearly, a few notes and guidelines are in order here. I would hate to be responsible for setting the Northwest on fire as readers surge out in an orgy of flaming zeal and blast their gardens (or neighborhoods) to history.

First of all, flame weeders are considered very safe by the agricultural industry. These tools are widely used among commercial growers of all sorts of things, from wine grapes to baby salad greens. Flamers are especially popular with organic growers because they use no toxins, leave no residues, and don't harm the environment (except maybe when you get careless and set the garage on fire).

Contrary to popular belief, flamers don't kill weeds by burning them. What they really do is dehydrate plants, in a big way. Plants, like us, are mostly water. When we flame weeds, the searing heat causes the water that fills their cells to boil. First the cell walls swell, then they burst, causing instant dehydration. It takes approximately two to three seconds of direct heat to accomplish this. (That's also why pouring boiling water on weeds is so effective.)

These gizmos are not just a propane torch on a stick. Most garden flamers consist of a 400,000 Btu propane vapor torch with an attached nozzle to direct the flames. Usually, they run off small (three- to ten-gallon) propane tanks. The flamer-operator lugs the propane tank around in a backpack, controlling the flame intensity with a handheld valve. This regulates the flow of propane so you don't freeze up your tank. (Propane freezes quickly when fuel is used too fast or when the fuel level in the tank drops too low.)

The idea is to suit up, then cruise the driveway, gravel path, or brick walk and give all unwanted plants a quick one-two. In the vegetable garden, you can flame over the whole planting area a day or two before your first seedlings are due out of the ground. Brand new vegetable babies are vulnerable to heat, but once they are up and growing well, you can flame away all competition.

Flamers are not much use in densely packed ornamental beds, but they are swell at cleaning up the ragged edge of a meadow border. Flaming does a fine job on broad-leaved weeds but won't kill most grasses without multiple heat treatments. Deeply taprooted weeds like dock and thistles also require several return visits.

Slugs also dehydrate quite quickly when exposed to an open flame. I have been fascinated by the mixed response to this news. Some readers are obviously inspired by it and can't wait to strap up and flame on. Others act horrified, even when I point out that cutting a slug in half with secateurs (the usual preferred disposal method) is no more humane than holding a teenie-weenie roast. Especially when you return half an hour later and snip up all the ex-slug's cannibalizing buddies.

If it comes to that, what slugs do to defenseless plants is not exactly humane. Slugs may be slow, but plants are even slower. Imagine what it feels like to be chewed to a skeleton by a slowly slithering slime bag, with no way to run. Most gardeners kill slugs only to protect their gardens. It's not a blood sport. It's not even a slime sport. It's simply a redistribution of nitrogen, in favor of the plants.

Remember, when you are dealing death, that the native banana slugs (the Really Big Yellow Guys) prefer rotting foliage to fresh. Their role is to clean up the forest floor, assisting the breakdown of leaves and whatnot. Think of them as compost makers. They are on your side (mostly). Indeed, Pete Ray, a nursery owner on Vashon Island, Washington, recently sent me my new favorite bumper sticker. Bright yellow and shiny with a lamination reminiscent of slug slime, it says Catch and Release Banana Slugs. Like wild trout, they deserve our assistance rather than harassment.

Garden flamers

Combatting slugs

The Euro-trash imports, on the other hand, are devastators of the first order. Brown, black, or gray, plain, stippled, or striped, these voracious herbivores are major garden pests. Whether you are trying to grow food crops or flowers, these little buggers are *not* on your side.

So yes, slug killing is interference with nature. So is weeding. So is having a garden. So is eating . . . the list is endless. Gardeners are, of course, free to allow slugs to roam unhindered through their gardens. But please don't complain when your plants look like green doilies.

If you decide to join the flame weeders, please read on. Hot tips passed on by enthusiastic flamers include wetting down house walls and wooden fences before flaming nearby weeds. Similarly, several readers who garden near open meadows report that using a sprinkler while flaming a garden discourages accidental brushfires.

Experienced flamers also reiterate that the weeds are killed by dehydration, not incineration. A three- or four-second blast is enough to do the trick, though it may take a day or two for the damage to show. Small broadleaved weeds will be done in immediately, but older weeds may require several heat treatments.

Most grasses are not killed by heat, which makes sense when you think about natural grasslands. Swept almost annually by wildfires, prairies and savannahs bounce right back from the ashes. An exception to this rule is weed grasses growing in gravel paths. When the paths are backed by weed cloth, roots can't penetrate very far. Small, shallow-rooted grasses growing in gravel paths can be killed by flame weeding. Grasses growing in rock walls seem similarly vulnerable.

In my garden, the beds are so thickly planted and deeply mulched that few weeds get a chance to infiltrate. I pull tiny weeds all winter and spring, until the borders grow too full to enter. Blankets of composted manure look as handsome as peat but are less apt to crust over. (When peat dries out, it becomes almost impenetrable to water, so plants mulched with peat can die of thirst in the rain.)

The worst problems arise where weedy meadow plants try to muscle in. The mixture of running grasses, wild buttercup, oxeye daisies, and various clovers looks pretty in the meadow but is a nightmare in garden beds. One year, I gave in and had a friend spray a large section with what is supposed to be an environmentally acceptable herbicide (Round-up). It did kill the grasses and most of the broadleaved herbs, but didn't touch the running clovers and buttercups.

Left unchallenged, these spread with enormous glee. I finally got them out (I think!) with my trusty hori-hori. This is my preferred hand tool, a heavy iron knife favored by Japanese farmers. Serrated on one side, the blade is strong enough to rip out interlaced colonies of clovers and buttercups. Use the sharp tip to unzip the long buttercup sideshoots, which root as they wander.

I think buttercups are beautiful, with their glazed petals and lacy, spotted leaves. Were they less territorial, I might admit them to parts of the garden. However, they are total oinks: They don't share, only take. Banned to the open meadow for bad behavior, they spangle the grass with their small suns. There they meet their match in the oxeye daisy. This, too, is a greedy creature that rolls over anything in its way. I root them out mercilessly in the garden, but leave them in the meadow to keep the buttercups in check.

As we have seen, flame weeders have a solid and respected place in the garden. Use them with care and they can assist garden maintenance quickly and without pollution. However, as (or if) summer dries up weeds and grasses, pay close attention to where that flame goes. Keep a hose nearby, and check the weeded area for smoke before leaving. As Smoky said, "Only you can prevent forest fires."

If you can't round one up locally, garden weeder flamethrowers are available by mail order through the Peaceful Valley Farm Supply.

As for slugs, well, recent years have been banner ones for mollusks. Most years, I only use metaldehyde bait (like Corry's) for a few weeks in spring. Once the plants are out of the ground, they are usually fine. The remaining slugs can be controlled with ammonia/water sprays. I still bait certain plants, and off several hundred slugs a day, on average, during the season.

One summer, when the great globular heads of ornamental onions (*Allium giganteum*) started lolling drunkenly, I discovered that their bases had been gnawed away by dozens of hungry baby slugs. Huge eremurus stems as thick as my wrist were similarly damaged. In both cases, thriving slug nurseries had been established amid the basal foliage. I slipped a handful of slug pellets into the leaf nodes, and hundreds of potential problems were abaited, so to speak.

In the cool of the evening, slugs come out to feed by the score. Those whose flaming skills have been honed can work off their emotional response to slug damage by blasting the slimers into the past. Just remember not to get too wild or you may scorch more garden plants than pests.

The best place to blast slugs is on a rock wall, where they congregate in the damp crannies. As they slither out in the gloaming, you can send them straight to slug heaven. If you are a heat weenie, the best hand-to-hand technique is to snip slugs in half with clippers. By the time you've made the rounds once, all the ex-slug's buddies will be feasting merrily on the remains. Dispatch them as they graze on the fallen, and keep going as long as your stomach holds out.

RESOURCES

PEACEFUL VALLEY FARM SUPPLY
PO BOX 2209
GRASS VALLEY, CA 95945
916/272-4769

Renewing Spring Mulches

 February

Over the years, I have written about heaping my garden beds in spring and fall with aged or composted manure. On new beds in particular, I may layer on as much as eight or ten inches for top dressing. I have also frequently discussed renewing the mulches in springtime, adding a fresh layer where winter rains had washed away the old stuff. Some have wondered about all this mulching. Did I mean that twice a year, each year, they should be adding eight to ten inches of compost and manure to the beds? Wouldn't the plants be smothered?

That's a good question, and yes, many plants would be smothered by a biannual blanket that deep. Not all, of course; you would most likely have a bumper crop of nettles and blackberries if you tried to blot those rowdies out with a blitz of bark. Most garden plants, however, are less determined and would probably be killed fairly quickly by so much of a good thing at once. A few would love it, so long as it was their kind of mulch. Many clematis are terrific rooters that don't mind having their necks buried in a loose, humusy mulch such as sifted garden compost or composted manure. Indeed, they will often make masses of extra side roots in response, greatly strengthening their ability to withstand drought and damage.

Grafted roses should be planted deep and mulched deeply as well. The bulky, bulging thickening on the stem above the roots is the graft union, which should be covered when the rose is planted. Deep planting and extra mulch encourage grafted roses to develop their own roots, reducing the chance of competition from the rootstock. Roses are also gross feeders, so they love a goopy mulch of aged manure and compost. In spring, I give each rose a double or triple handful of alfalfa pellets (the kind used as goat food) for an added boost of nitrogen. When alfalfa is combined with manure, the nitrogen release from both substances is synergistic, and the roses reap the benefit with greedy pleasure.

In perennial beds, the mulch is generally only a few inches deep, because the plants are quite closely spaced and it's vital not to smother their dormant crowns with wads of wet manure just as they are trying to wake up. What's more, many perennials do not take kindly to heavy mulch in any season and will rot away in protest if excessively covered. In my old garden, spring mulch renewal consisted mostly of fluffing and grooming the mulch. In the new one, it involves replenishing humus lost to summer sun and winter downpours (we had almost a foot of standing water in parts of the garden its first winter). In any case, during a mulch-spreading session, low spots are filled in, high ones leveled out, and

Feeding mulches and weeding mulches

any thin spots are renewed. In new beds, where there are still gaps left for expansion of young plants, I do pile mulch on more thickly to keep nosy weeds from finding unfilled spots. However, the total depth of established perennial border mulch will rarely be more than two to three inches.

There are, of course, exceptions. In my meadow border, where infiltrating weeds are a constant problem and the border plants being mulched are large, well rooted, and sturdy, I use mulch far more generously. An average depth is perhaps six or eight inches, and in bad spots where no detailed plantings have yet been made, I dump barrowloads of dry bark to a depth of two feet. Again, I take care to keep the plants' crowns only thinly covered, which means tapering that mulch blanket into a bowl shape around each plant.

The nature of the mulch makes a big difference and should always be taken into consideration. Light, open, airy mulches, like sieved compost and commercially pit-washed or composted manure are the best choices around small plants, particularly young or delicate perennials. Fine- or medium-ground bark works well in shrubby plantings or the woody backs of deep mixed borders. Coarse-ground bark is best for paths or around good-sized trees and shrubs, where there is no danger of smothering or squashing babies with the big lumps. No matter what you mulch with, be sure that both the planting bed soil and the mulching substance are at least damp. After all, one main benefit of properly placed mulch is the conservation of soil moisture. To avoid desiccating your plants (or even creating a fire hazard in dry summer areas), never heap dry mulch on dry soil. This is rarely a problem in spring, when finding a dry day to work in the garden can be a challenge. In autumn, however, if mulching is done before the fall rains return, it can create problems. Research (and direct experience) shows that plants that go into winter dry are more susceptible to a whole range of troubles and are not infrequently killed. In a drought year, deep mulches will actually form a barrier to moisture. Instead of protecting plants' resources, the mulch actually wicks moisture from the soil. What's more, many mulch materials are difficult to rewet once utterly dry. Once they crust over, rain runs off instead of penetrating.

In my garden, I spend the delicious early spring weekends doing mulch duty and filling in those adorable divots the deer leave behind. When they leap in their carefree way through the beds, our clever island deer manage not only to break and chew a lot of top growth but to gouge great holes in the soil as well. They are not alone in this. Dogs also leave deep footprints in the wet, soft soil of winter. The meanderings of the two Newfoundlands next door can be traced easily by the gigantic depressions they leave behind as they wander through the new beds. So can the cute little sneakers of errant neighborhood children looking for shortcuts or lost toys. So, in fact, can the size eight boots of the gardener in search of an empty place to put new plants.

The upshot is that winter leaves the average garden bed looking like a minefield. Come spring, all of those various kinds and sizes of holes need to be filled in and smoothed over. Empty spots where annuals once rested or where malcontent plants of any description flew the coop also need leveling off. Since wet soil is as soft as a sponge, I tend to wait until the ground has had a chance to dry out a little before renewing the mulch. (Some years, of course, that means waiting until July.) When it does dry out sufficiently to be worked, I begin planting and grooming simultaneously. Each time I plant something new, I work the area around it as well. Low spots are evened up with compost and aged manure, and high ones are smoothed down.

After major weeding sessions, I add that much-discussed fresh coat of mulch. As you will have gathered, its purpose is multiple: to suppress any new weeds that might be thinking about sprouting, to prevent spring mud from splashing my emerging bulbs, to conserve summer moisture, and more immediately to improve the look of the borders. Just as making the bed improves the appearance of a bedroom, a tidy spring mulch makes borders and beds look full of potential instead of rumpled and half-empty.

MARCH

Hardy Marginals
Survive the Wettest Winters

 March

After one of the soggiest winters in recent memory, it feels extremely pleasant to once again garden without the accompaniment of the endless rain. The recent spate of lengthy sunbreaks made it possible to explore the garden at leisure. I had been wondering how many plants survived the ongoing deluge, and the answer was surprisingly good.

In these parts, we are very apt to lose plants to winter wet long before they suffer from cold. This particular winter had offered opportunities to succumb to both, yet a heartening number of borderline tender plants were back and ready for another season of bloom. In very young gardens like mine, plants that have been in the ground only a few months often lack the sturdy roots that could get them through hard winters. Humus, in the form of compost and aged manure, is the usual recommended substance to encourage root growth, and it certainly does. However, the addition of lots of coarse grit or builder's sand makes an equally enormous difference if you are dealing with heavy clay soils, which may hold water to the exclusion of air.

Plant roots need both and can literally drown if the groundwater level remains too high for too long. Adding lots of grit to each planting hole improves the immediate drainage but can't help when standing water saturates the ground. One solution is to grow rot-susceptible plants in raised beds or large containers. Another, simpler idea is to seek out plants that don't mind wet feet in winter. Lots of bog plants qualify, of course, including the beautiful golden skunk cabbage and the pleated fans of *Veratrum nigrum*, our native false hellebore.

However, unless you have a real bog or seep to offer, most water lovers will resent our usual summer drought. To avoid extra watering in summer, we can experiment with hardy marginals, plants that inhabit lake, stream, and river margins. Some, like bog dwellers, need wet feet all year round. However, those that occur on sloping banks and higher ground generally tolerate wet soils in winter and drier ones in summer, since that's exactly what they get in their native habitats.

I recently became actively interested in this large class of plants, thanks to my present garden. Set on a rolling hillside, it is threaded with small seeps, tiny streamlets that are not always visible on the soil surface. A combination of bog plants and hardy marginals gave me a splendid palette of plants to choose amongst. Indeed, this adaptable group of plants can solve a number of common garden difficulties. In water gardens, hardy marginals are traditionally grown in pots sunk just beneath water level. In gardens, many will do just fine in a well-drained, open-textured soil. For instance, water forget-me-not (*Myosotis scorpioides*) ruffles along just as happily in a border as in a pool or pond. A long bloomer, this scrambler comes in clear, summer-sky blue as well as the deeper 'Sapphire' and charming if sappily named 'Pinkie'.

Where robust plants with sculptural lines are wanted, consider the giant reed grass, *Arundo donax*. It can get over twelve feet tall in damp places, and even reaches eight or ten feet in drier soils. Grown in damp ditches throughout France, this great grass is the source for clarinet and other woodwind reeds. In the garden, it needs plenty of room to stretch out and should not be paired casually, for it will quickly overwhelm less self-assured companions. The outsized Joe Pye Weed, *Eupatorium fistulosum* 'Gateway', whose fat flower heads look like grape-colored balloons, is another big plant that can stand up to the reed grass and indeed contrasts attractively with it in form and line. Both will grow in many situations, but give of their best when offered good, deep soil enriched with lots of humus.

A queenly cardinal flower, *Lobelia* × 'Red Giant', is another statuesque creature, topping out at about ten feet in mucky soils. Its multiple stems don't need staking and are covered with hot red flowers from late summer into fall. It needs a lot of elbow room, and its clear, clarion red is not the best mixer in amongst the usually quiet tones of the shade garden. However, place it where those red flowers catch a streak of afternoon or morning sun, and the effect becomes truthfully breathtaking. The jolt of pure color comes as a stimulating shock after so much gentle tastefulness.

Water in the soil encourages lots of the creeping veronicas, and when I saw *Veronica beccabunga* in the hardy marginal listings, I had to have it. I grew this years ago from seed, feeling that anything with so silly a name deserved a trial. It eventually died out in the drier beds of the old garden, but here, in the luxuriance of mud, it has capered its way through all sorts of larger plants, weaving a tight, glossy green carpet studded with cobalt blue blossoms. Where the soil is richest, the green mats climb to the dizzying height of a foot, but elsewhere, they stay low and lacy, clambering around the base of my skunk cabbages and the native *Veratrum californicum*.

Bog plants and hardy marginals

Water forget-me-not

Giant reed grass

Joe Pye weed

Lobelia ('Red Giant')

Skunk cabbage

Creeping veronica

Purple thalia

Brugmansia

Daturas

I loved skunk cabbages as a child and was pleased to learn that the western version, *Lysichiton americanus*, glowed just as brightly as the eastern one I grew up with, *Symplocarpus foetidus*. In England, these handsome, sculptural plants are grown in damp borders, where they are admired as bog lilies. I thought the idea terrific and am now growing both the golden-hooded *Lysichiton* and the white

Russian, *L. camtschatcensis*. Both take time to develop into good-sized plants when seed grown, but a number of nurseries are offering seed-grown plants these days. This is far better than pillaging the wild for larger plants, which rarely adapt well to garden settings.

I'm also experimenting with purple thalia, a sturdy three- to four-footer with long, paddle-shaped leaves like those of a canna, but flushed with a pewtery sheen of blue-gray. Thalia's flowers are held at the tips of long, flexuous wands, reminding me of a wetland angels fishing rod (*Dierama pulcherrimum*). Soft, lapping bracts of muted, dusky purple surround the tiny flowers, which hang in globular clusters from those long, arching stems. This is a Gulf States native that may not be hardy here without the protection of two feet of water. I'm going to take a chance that we'll have a mild enough winter to let it get established. So far, the thalia seems happy to bury its feet in the goopy soil in my sunny bog. Come late fall, I'll pile some bracken on the crown for frost protection, and assuming (perhaps foolishly) that neither deer nor mice will feast on its starchy roots, I'm thinking it should pull through nicely. We'll see.

After all, despite difficult winters, we do have some amazing survivals. Perhaps the most astonishing plant was the exotic, tropical-looking *Brugmansia* × 'Charles Grimaldi', a *Datura* relative with enormous leaves and foot-long, salmon-pink flowers. Fluted and swirling, they hang off the branches, giving a spirited impression of a dress shop patronized by Ginger Rogers, who wore similarly confectionery garments while tripping the light fantastic with Fred. In their South American homeland, brugmansias are trees and large shrubs. Here, greenhouse specimens can achieve ten to fifteen feet in a season and bloom all year round. In the open garden, they make an eight- to ten-foot shrub and don't bloom until late summer and fall.

Both brugmansias and daturas come easily from cuttings, so the summer before I minced an elderly one and stuck pieces of stem all over the garden. The slugs ate the smaller ones, but a good dozen survived, growing especially lush in the wet spots. After winter bouts with snow and frost, I assumed they were all dead and began to pull the stumps. However, I was tickled to find healthy live roots deeper down, with a few green shoots breaking from the woody old base. I baited around the crown to protect it from those voracious slugs, and sure enough, by midsummer we had a good-sized shrub dangling with long, peachy buds.

If you want to research bog plants and hardy marginals yourself, many are available at local water garden nurseries. If you can't find specific ones, or are interested in a greater selection, write to Crystal Palace Perennials for a complimentary catalog. (So far, this is the only known source for the giant red lobelia.)

RESOURCES

CRYSTAL PALACE PERENNIALS
PO BOX 154
ST. JOHN, IN 46373

Biodiversity in Danger

 March

All over the world, unique and often unknown plant species are vanishing at an alarming rate, never to return. The result of this ongoing loss can only be guessed at, but it scares botanists and food scientists silly. Ever hear of the Irish potato famine? During the 1840s a blight wiped out the entire potato crop in Ireland, costing a million and a half lives. Why? Because every one of those potatoes was genetically identical, a successful and popular agricultural strain that had replaced the myriad kinds grown until the recent past.

Since that initial disaster in Ireland, there have been worldwide wheat blights, and corn blights, and rice blights, each one life threatening and economically devastating. Every time, the search for resistant strains involves thousands of species, perhaps only one of which shows resistance to the disease. *Genetic Time Bomb*, a documentary produced by Oregon Public Broadcasting (order information on page 56), examines the ways in which genetic diversity is endangered and protected around the globe.

Although this issue has only recently achieved national attention, it has engaged plant scientists for over a century.

In Russia, for instance, one of the world's oldest seed banks commemorates Nikolai Vavilov, a passionate plantsman whose vision sparked an international movement to preserve biogenetic diversity. During World War II, Vavilov was imprisoned, yet his colleagues starved to death at their desks during the siege of Leningrad rather than eat the thousands of pounds of grains and beans that surrounded them. They believed that the legacy of seeds was more important than preserving their personal lives.

Unfortunately, few humans share this attitude. Loss of habitat, pollution, and desertification claim a huge toll of plant species every day. Plant breeders fear that too soon diseases will rampage unchecked because we will have lost the plants that could supply resistance. Worldwide, despite the increasing losses, government funds for seed preservation and research dwindle each year.

Fortunately, there is hope. *Genetic Time Bomb* also introduces us to a number of grassroots groups that actively protect thousands of endangered seed strains and species. Some of these groups will be familiar to gardeners who like experimenting with old-fashioned vegetables and fruits, which are often more flavorful than modern types bred for their superior packing qualities. Seed Savers Exchange in rural Iowa keeps thousands of heritage vegetables alive through its network of volunteer growers. In New Mexico, an alternative seed company called Seeds of Change offers an extraordinary selection of heritage vegetables, all organically grown and open-pollinated. More than five hundred varieties of vegetables, grains, herbs, and garden flowers are listed each year, and the workers grow thousands of other endangered strains as well.

Protecting endangered seed strains and species

If this topic leaves you feeling worried about our shrinking biogenetic heritage, take heart. The addresses of several such organizations are included below. Your contribution to them will make even more plant protection possible. What's more, any of us with a few feet of ground to spare can help out directly by growing one or two of these heritage strains and passing the seed on to others. If only 10 percent of this country's forty million gardeners were to do this on a regular basis, we could vastly improve the outlook for genetic preservation. It's as easy as sharing what we grow, something most gardeners are already very good at.

We can also find comfort in the increase of plant and seed catalogs that offer a wide variety of seeds from all over the world. The Cook's Garden offers a world tour of salad greens, European squash, and heirloom tomatoes renowned for savory flavor. Shepherd's Garden Seeds stocks Finnish as well as Italian favorites, and has more Japanese and Chinese greens and vegetables than most of us have ever dreamed of. J. L. Hudson, the fabled seedsman whose catalog is crammed with thousands of rare and obscure plants, sells a fat, ninety-five-page booklet called the Ethnobotanical Catalog of Seeds for a dollar. In it are listed hundreds of plants, including edibles and medicinals, that have been used by people in many times and cultures. Books, videos, and magazines are also sold through these pages, which are packed with an awe-inspiring quantity of information.

Even more hopeful is the fact that many mainstream nursery companies are getting on the bandwagon as well. Burpee has bolstered its modern seed stocks with a catalog called Burpee Heirlooms, which sells heritage fruits and vegetables as

RESOURCES

SEED SAVERS EXCHANGE
3076 NORTH WINN ROAD
DECORAH, IA 52101
$25 ANNUAL MEMBERSHIP FEE;
3 ANNUAL MAGAZINES/SEED LISTS

SEEDS OF CHANGE
621 OLD SANTA FE TRAIL, #10
SANTA FE, NM 87501
CATALOG $3
505/438-8080, FAX 505/438-7052

SHEPHERD'S GARDEN SEEDS
30 IRENE STREET
TORRINGTON, CT 06790
860/482-3638, FAX 860/482-0532
CATALOG FREE

THE COOK'S GARDEN
PO BOX 535
LONDONDERRY, VT 05148
800/457-9703
CATALOG FREE

BURPEE HEIRLOOMS
WARMINSTER, PA 18974
800/487-5530
CATALOG FREE

J. L. HUDSON, SEEDSMAN
ETHNOBOTANICAL
CATALOG OF SEEDS
STAR ROUTE 2, BOX 337
LA HONDA, CA 94020
CATALOG REQUESTS ($1):
PO BOX 1058
REDWOOD CITY, CA 94064

GENETIC TIME BOMB
OREGON PUBLIC TELEVISION
800/475-2638

seed or plant starts. Look over the list included here, order up some catalogs, and get growing. Even if you try only one antique form this year, and even if you save only a little seed from one plant, and even if you pass that seed on to only one friend or neighbor, you will be making a difference. The problem is frighteningly complex, but our part of the solution is that simple.

Blue Pandas and Purple Passions

 March

One of the hottest new perennials to appear in years is *Corydalis flexuosa* 'Blue Panda', a lacy, foot-high confection with delicate, ferny foliage and a luxuriance of sky blue flowers. Like its more common cousin, yellow-flowered *Corydalis lutea*, it blooms in small plumes, the slim stems studded with tubular, birdy little blossoms like clustered doves.

Once you have seen 'Blue Panda' growing gloriously, you definitely want to try some for yourself. This handsome creature grows superbly at the Northwest Perennial Alliance Borders at the Bellevue Botanical Garden (BBG), where deep manure mulches encourage it to uncommon size and height. (Though the title of the borders is a mouthful, the borders themselves are mouthwatering. Do yourself a favor and visit if you have the chance.) The fabulous displays of 'Blue Panda' at the BBG had people saying that this terrific new plant would soon replace forget-me-nots, since the color is richer, the bloom season is longer, and the overall form of the plant is far superior. What's more, corydalis is a solidly hardy perennial.

This initial enthusiasm has been tempered by experience, however. Though a strong grower when happy, 'Blue Panda' can be finicky in the garden. When it first appeared in the early 1990s at astronomical prices, this plant caused a lot of heartache by dying off as soon as it was transplanted. Now we know that compact plants from four-inch pots transplant better than large, overly lush ones in gallons. We know that greenhouse-coddled plants need careful hardening off before they get introduced into soggy spring gardens. We also know that corydalis prefers dappled shade and open-textured, humus-enriched soils, rather than sun and drought or deep shade and dampness. It's not crazy about unamended clay under any circumstances. 'Blue Panda' also has the annoying habit of growing great for somebody else in exactly the conditions it detests in your garden.

Chinese corydalis

'Blue Panda'

'Purple Leaf'

'Père David'

'China Blue'

If 'Blue Panda' doesn't appreciate your yard, take heart. China has proved to be full of blue corydalis, many of which are filtering into our country via nurseryman Peter Ray, whose Puget Garden Resources was long the only source for several kinds. Thanks to Pete, lots of us have found consolation in growing a number of splendid forms of *Corydalis flexuosa* that are decidedly easier to please in the garden. Panda's cousins bloom in a range of blues, from sapphire to turquoise, with similarly dainty foliage tinted blue-green, copper, or dusky purple. This last, called 'Purple Leaf', arouses a particularly passionate response in colorists, who adore the way those deep blue flowers smolder against their subfusc backdrop. Each leaf is centered with a spreading stain the color of Concord grapes, which lifts the wine-blue flowers into prominence.

Peter Ray first imported several of the blue corydalis he grows from England, where he saw them growing best in light shade. ("Open woodlands seem to be ideal," he says.) He also recommends improving their soil with plenty of humus such as compost and aged manure. "They prefer well-drained soils but bloom a lot longer when they get a regular supply of water," he notes. "Don't keep them soaked, but don't let them dry out either."

Though fairly similar, each form has its own strength. Tallest and lustiest in constitution, *C. f.* 'A.M. Form' (to fifteen inches) has hot blue flowers that stand up well above their dark green filigree of foliage. A.M. stands for the Royal Horticulture Society's Award of Merit, which is not given to dogs. This is indeed a good plant, blending beautifully with soft drifts of our native *Tolmiea menziesii* 'Taff's Gold' and the pleated fans of native *Veratrum californicum* in a damp and shady corner of my new garden.

On the west side of the house, 'Père David' opens clusters of sapphire blue flowers in earliest spring. Named for a plant-hunting priest who botanized China when not busy saving souls, this one has a suitably sturdy habit and an adaptable disposition. I grow a little colony of 'Père David' nestled into a wide ruffle of native wood sorrel (*Oxalis oregana* 'Winter Form'), which has rosy magenta flowers and burgundy-backed leaves. Behind the corydalis rises a dark-flowered *Helleborus orientalis*, grown from seed from the Bellevue Botanical borders, whose oxblood red petals have a faint blue bloom on them, which is accentuated by the company of the good father.

When I planted my young garden, 'China Blue' was my favorite, and it appears in bands and ribbons through several beds. This gentle runner has coppery, olive green foliage and clear, porcelain blue flowers that carry across the whole garden. The east-facing bed is its favorite spot, and it luxuriates there in deep, manure-based soil amid a tangle of red-twigged dogwoods, evergreen *Iris foetidissima*, daphnes, and sweet box (*Sarcococca hookeriana*).

The lustrous 'Purple Leaf' is usually the first of the blues to blossom, opening its bobbing little bluebirds in late winter. They continue to arrive in little flocks through spring, kept company by a series of bulbous buttercups like *Ranunculus ficaria* 'Brazen Hussy', its cooler sibling 'Double Bronze', and the cheerful 'Green Petal' (all of which I wheedled from Pete Ray). In one spot, 'Purple Leaf' is paired with black mondo grass (*Ophiopogon planiscapens* 'Nigrescens'), whose strappy little runners poke their way into the corydalis fronds in delightful disarray. Neither plant seems to mind sharing turf this way, and both seem to relish the damp, shady setting, growing better in this north-facing, rather mucky site than anywhere else in the garden.

All of these *C. flexuosa* selections bloom from early or mid-spring into summer, repeating moderately if kept dead-headed and well fed. All are creepers, making wide clumps in a single season, slowly spreading into sizable mounds over time. All also shed their leaves in hot summers, dying away early and leaving gaps that require kindly screening. In the sunniest beds, I use a large malva relative, *Kitaibela vitifolia*, to perform this service. In spring, these robust plants leap from the ground as eagerly as any lavatera. However, they don't really spread their skirts until the corydalis have begun to fade. As they curtsy and bow themselves out, the kitaibelas bounce their way to center stage, where they happily produce clouds of white mallow blossoms well into fall. In shadier spots, a goodly collection of late rising arisaemas and pinellias veil the departing corydalis clumps, aided by hostas, rodgersias, and ferns.

In contrast, 'Blue Panda' blooms from midspring through the summer, with a few lulls during the hottest weather. Its clumps slowly enlarge but never break and run as the others do. These habits, and certain other differences, make some botanists question whether 'Blue Panda' might be a natural hybrid of *Corydalis flexuosa* with some other of China's many species, or even a new and different species altogether. Indeed, it is exciting to think about what treasures are still to come from the wilds of China, where further plant exploration has been forbidden until quite recently.

For instance, I once grew an as yet unnamed species from Chinese seed that has a lax habit, pale blue-green, cutleaf foliage, and glowing, bicolored flowers that are half sapphire, half smoky turquoise. This one makes a plump storage root, something like that of *Corydalis solida*. It came from—well, I'm not allowed to say where it came from, but because the director of the unnamed place was unguarded enough to admit that he had give one to Rosemary Verey, he had then no choice but to give one to me and my companion, Barbara Barton, as well. When I left my farmhouse garden, I passed it on to Pete Ray (see, these exchanges go both ways) and to Jerry Flintoff, the Seattle plantsman who selected *Pulmonaria*

'Roy Davidson' and 'Benediction', among other things. Thus do fine plants make their way into general circulation, which is good for all concerned.

The summer sky blue of Panda's flowers can also border on turquoise in certain soils. It's a marvelous tint, but not always an easy one to work with, as colorists quickly discover. Chartreuse lady's mantle (*Alchemilla mollis*) makes a splendid companion for anything of this hot blue, as does golden Chinese water grass (*Hakonechloa macra* 'Aureola'), which Panda pairs with at the Bellevue borders. The Pandas at the BBG borders are enormous, some approaching the size of bushel baskets, so they require sizable and shapely partners.

In my own experience, as at the BBG, the key to happy corydalis is manure. Some seventy yards of pit-washed dairy manure are incorporated into the Northwest Perennial Alliance (NPA) borders each spring. Taking the hint, I added lashings of aged manure to the planting holes when I set out my plants. I started with several flats of four-inch pots of half a dozen kinds of blue corydalis. I planted them out in October, and despite the rough winters, they have grown with exuberance (except the two plants that the neighbor's dog likes best, which simply underlines the value of well-*aged* manure as opposed to fresh).

RESOURCES

FOR MORE INFORMATION ABOUT THE NPA, CONTACT THE NORTHWEST PERENNIAL ALLIANCE
PO BOX 45574
SEATTLE, WA 98145-0574

TO VISIT THE BORDERS:
NORTHWEST PERENNIAL ALLIANCE BORDERS AT BELLEVUE BOTANICAL GARDEN
WILBURTON HILL PARK
12001 MAIN STREET
BELLEVUE, WA 98015-4536
425/452-2750
GARDEN OPEN DAILY FROM DAWN TO DUSK, VISITOR CENTER OPEN 10 A.M. TO 5 P.M. DAILY. ADMISSION IS FREE.

If you are wondering how to pronounce the family name, I can set your mind at rest. Some years ago, a group of us were debating this issue when we were interrupted by a quiet cough. "Excuse me, but the lady is correct," said Steve Antonow (now of Seattle, then of Chicago). "In Greek, of course, the antepenultimate syllable always takes the stress." I have never forgotten that since, and I bet you won't either. So: Cor-Y-dalis, got that?

Ladybug, Ladybug

 March

The invasion started slowly. After the new year, every warm day seemed to produce a little crop of ladybugs to decorate the south-facing windows in my house. At first, it was just a handful of critters, and I thought it was kind of cute. Then, however, the quantities escalated. Whenever the sun came out, my windows were covered with ladybugs. Not only that, but the floors were covered with them, too. Indeed, they crunched underfoot when I got up at a hideously early hour each morning to see my kids off to school.

Ladybugs are very welcome in my garden, where they do wonderfully destructive things to aphids. Ladybugs in the bedroom are another story. What was wrong with these little ladies? Didn't they know they were supposed to migrate to southern climes? Didn't they remember how great it was to experience winter dormancy in a nice big cave down south? It's hard to believe that anybody would find a winter on Bainbridge Island preferable to one in San Miguel.

Then I remembered seeing pictures in *National Geographic* showing how those migrating ladybugs get treated down there. It seems that they like communal dormancy, and in many places they gather so thickly that they can literally be shoveled into containers. Ever since the boom in organic gardening, there has been a steady market for hungry ladybugs. Gardeners plagued by aphids and the plant viruses they bring are happy to let the newly awakened ladybugs feast in their gardens. Maybe these girls were just saving themselves the aggravation of a long, weary trip and a rudely disturbed nap.

Like so many people in the Seattle area, I have learned to call on Sharon Collman when a question like this is bugging me. Collman, a longtime King County Extension Service Agent, is one of those people who slip into phone booths and emerge wearing a snappy costume and demonstrating super powers. Bug Lady, Collman's alter ego, has powers of observation most of us can only envy. What's more, her rapport with the natural world is such that bugs are wondrous rather than weird to her.

Even more impressive, Bug Lady has the ability to awaken a similar outlook in people whose appreciation for bugs has hitherto been deeply dormant. With her help, we see the world with new eyes. Even the smallest of its inhabitants has an important place in the grand scheme of things. Bugs are not just something to be squished out of hand, but busy creatures with agendas that as often coincide with ours as not. Once we figure that out, we can encourage them to act in concert with our ideas, rather than ignoring or actively harming them. Having any force of nature on your side is a good idea. When you consider that bugs make up more biomass than all of the mammal species put together, the concept of cooperation becomes even more attractive.

The idea that many insects are beneficial to gardeners and farmers is slowly gaining ground in this country, where nature is often viewed as ours to trample, abuse, or control. Bug Lady would like to see more people take the time to make a quick phone call before assuming that indoor bugs—or any bugs—are bad and offing them. "These particular ladybugs aren't natives, they're Asian imports," she explained. Though similar to our native ladybugs, they display a few fascinating differences. "As a species, *Harmonia axiritis* shows incredible variation," Sharon notes. "You can find red or orange ones with black spots, or black ones with red or orange spots, and red or orange or black ones with no spots. Some of them have lots of spots, some have fewer or none, but despite the apparent differences, they are all the same genetically."

Originally, the Asian ladybugs were released over in Yakima by the USDA, which was looking for benign controls on some serious aphid problems that insecticides couldn't touch. The imported ladybugs did a fine job of demolishing the crop-damaging aphids, and all was well. The only problem was that the Asian ladybugs didn't know where to go when migration time rolled round. Instead of winging their way south of the border, they found places to their liking in and around homes. Eventually, they made their way over the mountains, probably hitching rides in campers and trucks as slumbering passengers. Now they spend the summers cleaning up our gardens. When autumn arrives, they seek out cozy corners, massing on roofs and walls of sheds and houses. This unnerves many people, who fear that the little bugs may be damaging the walls in some way.

Dust-busting ladybugs

Resident ladybugs aren't hurting the house at all, Collman assures us, but dead ones can cause problems. "When people spray them and they die in the walls, they become food for carpet beetles, who won't eat live ladybugs but feast on dead ones. Now, these little buggers are everywhere. When we think our favorite sweater has been nibbled by moths, it's really been a snack for a carpet beetle. Those guys are way worse than the ladybugs, and do far more damage. To prevent encouraging big carpet beetle infestations, don't kill ladybugs indoors."

Not too surprisingly, carpets rank high among the carpet beetle's favorite treats, but so does natural fiber clothing. They love flour (they often live in uncovered flour sacks) and also eat bread and cookies. Indeed, those who leave their gingerbread houses around after the holidays often wonder who is chewing away at the foundations: Carpet beetles are the culprits. "Nobody worries about carpet beetles, because you never see them crawling over the coat hangers, making their way toward just the right sweater," says Collman. "Ladybugs are more visible, and they don't belong inside, so people panic when they find them out of place."

Ladybugs, however, are completely benign. "The worst thing ladybugs do is release a bitter scent when disturbed," comments Collman. "They are most apt to do it when they are stepped on, and how can you blame them? Oh, now and then they bite, but that's not very serious; it feels like having a single arm hair pulled. It really bothers people, though, because it's so unexpected. People who anthropomorphize critters feel a sense of betrayal when something that's supposed to be cute and gentle bites."

Why haven't the imports figured out how to migrate with their American buddies? Aren't they supposed to fly away home each fall? "These girls seem to prefer to winter over in our cozy houses and sheds," Collman says with a chuckle. When it warms up, they move toward the heat, trying to get out into the sun. However, most springs, it's still too cold out there for ladybugs when they first wake up in March

If the ladybugs are bugging you, Collman recommends collecting and storing them for another month or so. "Just put a clean bag in the dust buster, vacuum them up, and dump them in a glass jar with a little sprinkle of water," she advises. Don't soak them, or they might drown. They just need a tiny amount of water to survive, she adds. "They'll keep well in the refrigerator until late April or May. Then you can release them in the garden and they'll be ready to eat aphids like crazy."

For more information about living in harmony with *Harmonia* or bugs in general, Seattle and King County residents can call the Master Gardener hotline at 206/296-3440 between 10 A.M. and 4 P.M. Monday through Friday. Indeed, these highly trained folks are ready to tackle any question you can dish up about gardening, whether it's about pests, problems, plant identification, or how to do practically anything in the garden.

Spring Cleaning
and Exploratory Surgery

 March

The garden I have been creating at a friend's rented cottage is nestled into the woods to the north and east, but open on the other sides to a sloping meadow. It's a great setting that offers a variety of aspects and soil conditions. This means we can grow a wide range of plants, which is, after all, half the fun of gardening. Best of all, there will be places for sun lovers that hated my old shaded garden, so I can experiment with a whole new crowd.

First we put in the main beds and created wide, graveled paths, using a base of woven weed cloth underneath a mix of fine, unwashed gravel (with what they call "the smalls" left in). We also added a low retaining wall of chunky basalt in order to shape the existing steep slope into two more manageable beds. Next, dozens of trees and shrubs were planted, as well as hundreds of perennial companions.

At this point, a lot of people thought we were nuts and started asking pointed questions. I answered them all the same way: Sure, it's a rental house and we won't be here forever, but so what? I always said that it's more fun to be making a garden than to have one. When the time comes, we'll just make another one. After all, it really is the process of garden making that is so rewarding. It's great to visit gardens, but I am always struck by how fast a visiting group can move through even a large, complex garden. Looking at the best garden in the world is far less captivating than working happily in your own modest patch.

In any case, we made our garden and had a terrific time doing it. The next year, we started the next best stage, which is editing and fine-tuning. During spring cleaning, each bed was tidied up and remulched. As we did the usual maintenance chores, we also reassessed plant relationships. Some companions already needed to be rearranged in order to give everybody the right amount of room. In other cases, budding partnerships were broken up and the various components reassigned to more (or less) optimal locations. Some people worry that such adjustments, made so early in the garden's career, imply that they (or their garden designer) did something wrong in the first place. The truth is, even the best plans require such tweaking, because each site is unique.

Plants often behave just a bit differently in sites a mere ten feet apart. Take them across town and you can expect some behavioral adjustments to follow. Usually the differences are slight; perennials may flower a few days earlier or later, or perhaps their petal color will alter a shade or two. Sometimes, though, plants adapt startlingly well to a new home. A demure clumper that never wandered is suddenly spreading far and wide. A plant that rarely seeded elsewhere is casting its offspring all over the yard. A vine that could barely scramble up its old trellis is now rambling over to visit the neighbors.

If a plant simply isn't growing, your spring cleaning session should include exploratory surgery. Gently lift the whole rootball to see if any obvious cause presents itself. A common difficulty is a rootbound plant put in an undersized hole. The solution is to generously enlarge each planting hole, adding significant amounts of compost and aged manure to both the hole and the backfill. (That's the soil you took out with the plant.) If the roots are wound tightly and haven't grown outward, you'll have to rough them up a bit. Scuff them apart with fingers or a hori-hori (Japanese farmer's knife), gently breaking up those wiry root coils.

This rough procedure horrifies those who relate a little too closely to their plants. They imagine what such tough treatment would feel like to them and shudderingly decline to perform it for their babies. Really, though, this is misplaced kindness. Human intervention caused the problem, and human intervention is required to fix it. Rootbound plants can't help themselves. They need our tough love to set them free.

This principle was strikingly illustrated at a class I held at my fledgling garden school, which we later decided should have been called "Overcoming Your Fear of Roots." In this class, nursery owners Kelly Dodson and Sue Skelly (proprietors of Reflective Gardens Nursery in Poulsbo, Washington) demonstrated their favorite techniques for releasing rootbound plants. Soon, a class participant leapt up to show us how he used a Felco folding pruning saw (mine, I noticed) to slice open a recalcitrant hosta. I countered by cleaving a large daylily in two with an old kitchen knife. At that point, it was open season, and all kinds of constructive havoc took place.

Tidying up the garden

Releasing rootbound plants

The resulting ripping, tearing, slicing, and shredding of roots caused some mental trauma in a few of those present, until Kelly proved its value through a highly dramatic example. First, he showed us a huge, thriving plant in a gallon container, then another one just limping along. He explained that the big one had been repotted by him, using the robust techniques just demonstrated. The other had been repotted by a nervous new employee who didn't want to "hurt" the little plant. Kelly then tipped both plants out on a table, and we could plainly see the vigorous new roots on the "brutalized" plant. The other, in vivid contrast, still retained the size and shape of a four-inch pot. A few tiny roothairs had succeeded in penetrating the tightly knotted old roots, but the plant was clearly suffering. With this sterling lesson in mind, the next time badly rootbound plants come your way, take the plunge, jump in, and let yourself rip. Remember, turning those roots loose won't hurt the plant at all. That fierce-looking tugging and teasing simply wakes up slumbering and stunted roots and tells them it's time to get growing. Replant your patient quickly, in a freshly prepared planting bed or in pieces, using as many containers as necessary. Next, water it in well and stand back, because formerly repressed plants often put on a lot of growth in a hurry.

APRIL

Slug Wars

 April

During warm, accelerated springs, serious slug damage can happen overnight. The moment susceptible plants leaf out, they suggest a midnight snack to gastropods, slugs and snails alike. Fortunately, there are lots of ways to protect our gardens from the ravaging hordes.

The first step is to keep our plants well fed and cared for. Healthy, vigorous plants are significantly less likely to be attacked than weak, sickly ones. A few years ago, researchers asked jailed pickpockets to look at videos of ordinary people walking along city streets and identify potential victims. Though the thieves were unaware of their own motives, a subtle pattern soon emerged: People who looked depressed or timid were prime targets, while those who walked briskly and with confidence were rarely chosen. The plant kingdom works on similar lines; weaker plants somehow announce their vulnerability to pests and diseases alike.

If this sounds too weird, try a simple test. Next time you notice a single, stressed-out broccoli in an otherwise healthy row, or find that one petunia from a six-pack sulks while others bloom, dig up the laggard and check out its roots. Chances are excellent that you will discover an obvious physical problem (usually damaged or twisted roots). Wounded plants can be nursed along in pots or a cold frame if they are really worth the fuss. If not, put them quickly out of their misery rather than leaving them to attract garden thugs.

The second line of defense is a good offense. My preferred Slug Wars methods are direct. This may mean squishing them underfoot (by the hundreds, on a damp morning) or hand-to-hand combat (try those bamboo barbecue skewers—wow!). My stealth bomber method involves cruising the garden with a spray bottle holding two parts water and one part nonsudsing household ammonia. (The sudsing kind contains surfactants that make it stick to the plants and may burn leaves.) When you mix up the slug water, put the tap water in first, followed by ammonia. That way, you are less likely to splash your skin or clothing with full-strength ammonia. I always keep a gallon or so mixed up in a plastic milk jug, so I can reload at leisure, and I also keep squirt bottles at each house entry door.

Any kind of spray bottle will do, but those super squirt guns favored by the kids are the best delivery system around. I pay my boys a penny apiece for each score when they do slug patrol, and they often collect several bucks each before breakfast. Direct hits cause slugs to fizz up into little lumps of nitrogen, thus replenishing the garden. Certain plants (notably trilliums) may be burned by ammonia water, so knock slugs off delicate plants with a stick before bombing. Very large slugs do not always succumb; they can slough off their outer coating in a horrid, rust-colored blob of slime and emerge unscathed. These honkers should be cut in half to be sure that they are really doing their share of nitrogen recycling. Those tiny baby slugs are the worst in terms of doing damage, since they eat several times their weight in fresh vegetation in order to fatten up properly. They do not eat bait, so the only way to get them is to swish out the crevices of plants like the angelicas, where they congregate in the dim, cool recesses of the large leaf nodes at the attachment points on the stems. Large bulbs also offer these tempting spots, and if you find a lot of stem damage at the soil line on alliums, fritillaries, and so forth, try this prophylactic rinse each day and see if it doesn't help.

One friend called to say that she had been spraying the garden each night with gallons of ammonia water and she still had tons of slugs. Sadly, this fine technique is not preventative; after you've washed your plants, you can then go on to wax and buff them, but none of that activity will deter slugs even slightly. No, it takes that direct hit to make an impression on these garden terrorists.

Among passive preventions, beer is the all-time crowd pleaser. Indeed, in some gardens, every day is Oktoberfest, with little pans of beer enticingly arrayed beneath every hosta and daylily. Beer is indeed a splendidly attractive bait, but some people get so carried away they walk around with baited breath, not a recommended practice. (Think of the morning mouth—yuck.) Among the best ways to use beer is in little tubs with tops. You cut entry doors an inch or two up from the tub floor, just big enough for a slug to slime through. Fill them up with regular (Northwestern slugs are not picky, so don't waste that microbrew), then set them out under infamously slug-attracting plants like ligularias and *Angelica gigas*. These little slug huts are also a good way to place metaldehyde-based baits where they won't be attractive to birds and pets. Empty them out daily, and you will be both pleased and revolted at the results.

Another deservedly popular slug deterrent is diatomaceous earth, the finely ground remains of ancient, fossilized creatures. Their sharp edges keep on slicing and dicing soft slug stomachs when the gardener is unavailable. This stuff lasts forever (it's already a zillion years old) and doesn't wash away except in heavy rains, but if you do a lot of plant moving or heavy weeding, it does get scattered about, which greatly reduces its efficiency.

Among commercial baits, Corry's (which is mostly bran) is the least environmentally destructive, but should still be used with discretion and caution. In the garden, excess slug bait can kill birds or

Methods of defense against slugs

Ammonia/ water spray

Beer

Diatomacious earth

Commercial bait

Copper strips

even cats and dogs. In water systems, leached garden poisons can kill fish and aren't great for people, either. What's more, in wet years, big slugs can recover from a toxic dose by rehydrating as they stagger away through wet grass. Let's not encourage the selection of toxin-resistant slugs, please. If you must use bait, place a small amount close to the plant base, where it won't attract birds or cats (again, containers with slug slots are a great way to go).

Some gardeners swear by strips of copper, which actually electrocute slugs, thanks to their salt-based body chemistry. In tiny gardens, each bed can have a little copper fence, but in larger areas where hand picking is an impractical control, you are apt to fence as many slugs in as out. Still, copper strips can be very effective when wrapped around the base of plant racks, tables, or pots. They also work nicely along the door frames of greenhouses, cold frames, and so forth.

It is worth mentioning that native slugs, like the big yellow banana slugs, eat only dead or dying foliage and are an important part of the ecological chain in the woods and meadows. The real culprits are English or European field slugs, both the tiny brown or black ones and the big tiger-striped kind, which feast on growing gardens. We can protect the native banana slugs by not using bait in or near woodland verges and by selectively hand-killing slugs through daily patrols rather than adopting the large-scale, passive kill techniques such as scattering bait.

Coral Bells That
Deck the Garden Walk

 April

A morning coffee break stroll through the garden put me in mind of a sentimental song we sang in grade school. It had to do with lilies of the valley, now in full, fragrant bloom, and white coral bells that ring only when the fairies sing. Though not audible and only just coming into bud, my coral bells are undeniably a lovely sight. These are not the old-fashioned coral bells of the song but younger cousins, valued more for their extraordinary foliage than for their floral charms.

Actually, their floral charms are nothing to sneeze at, for many of the new coral bells bloom long and hard, sending up several sets of slender, elongated stalks tipped with airy sprays of small, nodding bells over the course of the summer. Their leaves, however, are their crowning glory for much of the year. (Despite the fact that many are nominally evergreen, their resting rosettes are seldom prepossessing in winter.) This new look is the result of patient hybridizing, most of it carried out by Oregonian Dale Heims. His introductions are just starting to reach the nurseries and garden centers, and all are snapped up as quickly as they appear. Heims's coral bells are belles indeed, some dramatically beautiful, others downright brazen.

Probably the best known of the foliage coral bells is

Heuchera micrantha 'Palace Purple', which has royal red leaves and white flowers. (It should, at least; too often, inferior seed-grown plants are offered instead of divisions of the true plant.) 'Palace Purple' was a chance seedling discovered in England when seed of our native Northwestern coral bell (*H. micrantha*) and an eastern species, *H. americana* (which tends to throw red seedlings), were both being grown near the Queen Mother's garden (thus the palace part). Handsome as it is, 'Palace Purple' is cast in the shade by most of Heims's hybrids.

I have grown an embarrassing number of these new coral bells over the past few years. When they first began to appear, they had for me that irresistible allure that certain species—pulmonarias, daylilies, iris, aconites—seem to project for collectors. You see one plant and grow it, falling more in love each passing day. You then learn that there are a whole lot more like that one back home. Where? How? Once bitten by a species bug, there is nothing for it but to have more. Indeed, some of us become so enthralled that nothing short of *all* will do. All available species. All available forms. All available selections. And what about the elusive, unobtainable, fabled forms? Why, you just have to find those as well. So what if you can't? You must. The quest for *all* becomes part of what fuels your life.

After a few cycles of this, the lucky begin to see the dark side of the pattern. Acquisition sickness is an addiction, and like any other addiction it becomes less satisfying rather than more. When you realize that half of those gotta-have-it plants are languishing, half dead, still in their pots, while you are still hot on the trail of yet another one, something snaps. I'm not going to fess up about how many plant lust cycles I spun through before figuring it out, but it did finally happen. For me, the turning point was the recognition that the concept of the plant had become more powerful than the real thing. That moment of clarity lead me to clean up my act, and with it my plant pile. It became a matter of pride to have everything planted, with nothing kicking around in pots. Oh, not all the time; what do you take me for? Still, at least twice a year, the potting ground must be empty.

Anyway, when it comes to coral bells, let me just say that I've grown my share and maybe your share as well. With that much exposure, some disillusionment is bound to creep in, and I can now say that all coral bells are not created equal. Some are truly fabulous plants and others are, well, let's say forgettable. At the moment, my personal favorite amongst the great ones is 'Chocolate Ruffles', a sumptuous creation with large lobed and scalloped leaves. When young, their edges are deeply ruffled, but older ones have a looser flounce, like a lettuce leaf hem on a chiffon skirt. The leaves are copper pink when young, maturing to a chocolaty green with burgundy veins and undersides. Its red flower stems set off its white flowers nicely. I have several large plants tucked beneath the skirts of *Spiraea japonica* 'Goldflame', a compact colorist's border shrub without peer. A color changer, its foliage begins life bronzed red, then turns to chartreuse before ending its season in a blaze of sunset shades. 'Chocolate Ruffles' calls out the copper in the spiraea foliage and also chimes elegantly with an understated *Carex plagellifera*, an auburn grass that manages to be both upright and flowing in form. Placed between two chocolate heucheras, the grass falls in a liquid tumble to the ground, broken only by the great seed heads of *Allium christophii*, some half dozen of which are allowed to remain in position until autumn winds toss them like tumbleweeds across the garden.

Coral bells

'Palace Purple'

'Chocolate Ruffles'

'Ruby Veil'

'Chameleon'

'Pewter Veil'

'Vera Jameson'

'Dale's Strain'

'Snowstorm'

My next favorite coral bell is the sultry 'Ruby Veil', whose similarly scalloped and shaped leaves are a dusty midnight red with fuchsia pink veins and backsides. Like so many of her kin (including 'Chocolate Ruffles'), Ruby makes foot-high mounds and produces rosy flowers on reddish, fourteen- to eighteen-inch stems. Some of the deeper-toned coral bells burn readily in sun, but here in the maritime Northwest, Ruby can take the heat and smolders attractively when given a sunny spot in rich soil. Ruby looks smashing when paired in a big pot with *Euphorbia dulcis* 'Chameleon', another new-comer on the scene. 'Chameleon' is a dusk-tinted, airy border spurge with upright new shoots and sprawling flowering stems that explode into puffy thunderclouds when they bloom. Where most euphorbia bracts are lime green, these come in murky shades of black and gray and slate and purple, taking on hotter tints of copper red and orange by late summer.

Seedlings appear everywhere in short order when you grow this enchanting spurge, and if you want to maintain a good, dark strain, it's important to rogue them, removing any that aren't potently colored in youth. On the other hand, the variability of the strain means that other fine plants are waiting to be recognized, just as with coral bells. I've begun separating young plants by color, putting the reddest youngsters together and moving blacker ones in their own group elsewhere. Coppery babies are also segregated, as are some peculiar brownish ones that look sort of putty colored now, but may reveal unsuspected beauties as they grow up. They may also prove to be utter dogs, in which case they will enrich the compost heap. I will have lost nothing by allowing them this trial, and perhaps — who knows? — the garden world may be minutely enriched as well, should any of these other shades prove gardenworthy.

The quietly stunning *Heuchera americana* 'Pewter Veil' is a subtler beauty with copper red new leaves that pass through several shades of bronze, red, and plum as they age. When mature, the leaves are heavily washed with gunmetal gray and veined in dim, old-growth-forest green, with hot pink backsides. In my new garden, this one is partnered with deer tongue ferns (*Blechnum spicant*) in a shady site, along with the dainty native foam flower, *Tiarella trifoliata*. This is a plant for those who enjoy details, for its small intricacies of leaf shape and pattern are lost to hasty observation. Tiarellas are closely related to heucheras, and indeed there are some intergeneric crosses that have resulted in attractive plants like rosy little *Heucherella tiarelloides* 'Bridget Bloom'.

'Pewter Veil' also grows happily in the sun next to a cascading *Sedum* 'Vera Jameson', which begins the season looking blue, then blooms in frosty shades of plum, lavender, and mauve. Like most of its kindred, this coral bell needs fairly frequent division to keep it in good looks. Mature plants tend to develop high, woody crowns with increasingly small leaves. When this occurs, dig the oldies up and let them collapse into many new plants. Those, long, woody-stemmed crowns aren't much use, but any younger ones can be pulled apart, and even those with few or seemingly no roots will take off quickly when stuck in good, well-drained but humusy soil. Plants in the ground seem to do better than those in pots, so set aside a small nursery area to ensure a steady supply of fresh young plants.

Most underrated of all is *Heuchera americana* 'Dale's Strain', a compact plant with delicate pink flowers and small, rounded leaves that are marvelously marbled. When young, the leaves are a matte chartreuse with olive green markings, while mature ones are silver green with spruce green veins. It does best in light shade and moderately moist soil. A shady spot is also best for *Heuchera* 'Snow Storm', a lusty plant with large, rounded leaves heavily dusted with clean white spots and spatters that can scorch in full sun. Its bright red flowers look like little firecrackers against the cool backdrop of its leaves, which make a wonderful counterpoint to broad-bladed hostas like the heart-shaped little 'Blue Cadet' or plain green *Hosta plantaginea*, with its sheaves of fragrant white flowers.

RESOURCES

COLLECTOR'S NURSERY
16804 NE 102ND AVENUE
BATTLE GROUND, WA 98604
CATALOG $2
OPEN BY APPOINTMENT ONLY:
360/574-3832

While most coral bells bloom best in full sun, many of our native species prefer the dappled shade of light woods or the meadow's edge. Since these newer hybrids often owe their distinctive patterning to native species, they all perform nicely in light or partial shade but may show signs of distress—browning or curling leaves—in full sun. Move the sufferer into a cooler spot and keep it moist and you should see healthy new growth appearing within a few weeks.

If you can't find these coral bells locally, nearly all can be ordered from Collector's Nursery, a small private nursery open only by appointment.

Blues and Bulbs

April

In April my garden is as blue as it can be. Mind you, I'm
not complaining; in the garden world, blues aren't bad.
Indeed, because blue flowers are relatively rare, having them
in the garden as frequently as possible is a favorite horticultural challenge. In some months, blue flowers are very hard
to come by (the winter months especially, unless you count
buds and late blossoms that are blue with cold, which I for
one do not). April, however, can bring, if not showers, at
least a bushel of blues to even the smallest garden.

A few shrubs offer the blues on a really big scale. The
springtime centerpiece of my blue and gold border is the
periwinkle blue azalea, *Rhododendron augustinii* (if that throws
you for a loop, just remember that azaleas are really a sub-
group of rhododendrons). This midsized shrub often has a
decidedly lavender cast, but the best garden forms are a soft,
smoky blue, the gentle color of a hazy midsummer sky. This
pleasing species has given rise to a number of even bluer
babies, such as 'Blue Diamond', 'Bluebird', and 'Blue Tit'
(we're talking birds here, not body parts). The first is nearly
as large as *R. augustinii* (to seven feet), while the other two
are low, slow-growing, and compact border rhododendrons.
There are blue rhododendrons for any situation, for lusty

evergreen hybrids like 'Blue Peter' will willingly fill a large corner in time, while diminutive 'Sapphire' will thrive for years in a container.

Lovely as these shrubs may be, the best of the blues are spilling all over the garden floor. Pools of primroses run in a dozen shades of blue, from cobalt through faded jeans to spring thundercloud. Chubby globes of *Primula denticulata*, the drumstick primrose, come in a warm range of lavender blues. They blend delightfully one into the other, or you can pick over the mixtures at the nursery to isolate the exact tints you prefer.

Another blue blossomed gang, the spotted lungworts (*Pulmonaria* species) are still in full flower as well. A handsome hybrid named for a famous Seattle plantsman, *Pulmonaria* 'Roy Davidson' has long, narrow, silver-spotted leaves and powder blue blossoms. The leaves get a little tired by late summer but hold their freshness far longer than a lot of lesser lungworts, so this is a good one for mixed borders where looks count all year round. So too is a new dazzler called 'David Ward', a creamy-edged, large-leaved fellow with sprays of peachy, apricot-colored flowers. He isn't blue, but he's sure pretty, and remains so all summer long if given good soil and a shaded spot. A true blue trooper, white-speckled 'Margery Fish' takes us back on target with her large clusters of tubular blooms the color of a clear spring sky. This plant has heavily frosted foliage, because the silvery spots are so close together she looks powdered with icing sugar.

Blue azaleas

Blue rhododendrons

Primrose

Allium

Spotted lungwort

Grape hyacinth

Blue windflower

Anemone

Bluebell

In some of her offspring, the silver merges and turns the leaves truly silver. If the flowers are as good as mom's, such babies can be keepers that might prove worthy of a name someday. Others, however, are simply speckled and spattered and have inferior flowers, and so are useful only for carpeting large expanses of ground until something better comes along.

The most striking blues of all come from minor bulbs. A few, like grape hyacinth (*Muscari armeniacum*), are old favorites that turn up in gardens uninvited, brought in on somebody else's coattails. This thuggy species is too rowdy to use in small gardens; instead consider the admittedly somewhat tender *Muscari moschatum*, whose dark little turrets are packed with purple-green blossoms that smell deliciously of ripe fruit. The muscari clan are quite common, but a surprising number of splendid little bulbs are still comparative unknowns. Long-lived, easygoing, inexpensive, and exceptionally floriferous, the blue minor bulbs are hard to beat.

One of my particular pets is blue windflower (*Anemone blanda*). Sheets of this charming little Mediterranean bulb appear everywhere in my garden, children of a hundred bulbs I planted some five years ago. They love the heavy clay, and have seeded themselves into generous drifts. I help the spreading process along by shaking the fuzzy seed heads wherever I want more of their starry flowers and lacy leaves. These happy creatures begin blooming in late winter and carry on well into spring. They also come in white, or pink, or rose, as well as in mixtures. The expensive named form called 'Blue Star' is too harsh in color for my taste, but the fairly cheap blend called 'Blue Shades' offers a delicious range of blues that tend toward the hazy, rather gray blue of bluebells. This wash of blues complements any other color you place it near, from gaudy golds and yellows to bright, singing reds and purples. It adds pop to pastels and softens the high, hot colors that sometimes need a little tempering lest they look like stray Easter eggs rather than garden flowers.

Larger florist's anemones (*A. coronaria*) are also starting to blossom now. These make big, silky poppy flowers, their smudgy black eyes trimmed with thick black fringe that gives them a luxurious depth and brilliance of color. They are often sold in color mixtures like 'De Caen', my own favorite with big, single flowers, or 'St. Brigid' (ruffled doubles), or the brash beauties called 'Tecolote Giant' (really big singles). To get the blues, grow these mixtures in a nursery bed until they show their true colors, then move them into the garden in groups of like tints. Keep your eye out as well for nurseries or catalogs that stock named hybrids like dark blue, single 'Mr. Fokker' or semidouble, ocean blue 'Lord Lieutenant'.

Those beloved old grape hyacinths are often found in older gardens, for they are ardent and persistent multipliers. This makes them excellent candidates for wild or meadow gardens, but they are slightly less welcome where space is at a premium. Several of their cousins are just as brightly blue and just as sweet smelling, yet are better behaved in mixed company. Two-toned *Muscari latifolium* sends up fat spikes of charcoal blue flowers with bright blue tips, an elegant partner for saucy golden avalanche lilies (*Erythronium species*) and the hot orange petals of Welsh poppy (*Meconopsis cambrica*). A plump grape hyacinth called 'Blue Spike' has curly, open blossoms instead of trim little bells, while *Muscari comosum* 'Plumosum' looks like fluffy blue feathers.

April is squill season as well. Drooping, mountain-lake-blue bells are dangling now from the slender stalks of *Scilla siberica*, a small charmer that will colonize freely under the skirts of deciduous shrubs like coppery *Spiraea japonica* 'Lemon Lime' or silver-splashed *Kerria japonica* 'Variegata'. For a softer effect, encircle a white 'Jet Trail' quince with a broad ribbon of striped squill, *Puschkinia scilloides* var. *libanotica*. This one is a bit taller, with soft spikes of clustered bells in tender, milky blue with turquoise stripes.

RESOURCES

DUTCH GARDENS
PO BOX 200
ADELPHIA, NJ 07710

Nearly all of these engaging little bulbs can be found in the Seattle area. At Tulip Festival time, Skagit Valley nurseries do a land-office business selling bulbs of all kinds. However, if you can't track down a particular pet, all of the bulbs mentioned here can be ordered very reasonably from Dutch Gardens.

Garden Giving

 April

Recently, an extremely generous gardener offered me a lot of good-sized plants free for the taking. Having been on both ends of this kind of offer, I knew that the proper response was to get in there with a shovel as soon as possible. Many people respond to such an offer with diffidence, assuming that to take you up on it is greedy. Well, perhaps it is, a bit, but our acquisitive side is what creates the expanded palette of the garden artist. (How's that for an excuse to buy plants?) Besides, it's usually the offering gardener's fascination with new plants that necessitates the removal of the outgrown. Welcome to the club.

Please remember this, however: Taking up a sincere offer of plants promptly is genuinely helpful. When you are ready to rearrange the garden, it's wonderful to let the hot wave of inspiration propel you forward to action. It's quite annoying to have to wait until somebody else has done their bit.

If you have promised plants to somebody and they seem to want them, it creates a cross-obligation. Now you have to leave the silly things in place until the new owner shows up to take possession. Or do you? The patient and kindly may let their giveaways ride for quite a while, but if the donor is a quick worker or impulsive, you'd better hustle those plants home.

Working on this theory, I spent the next weekend with a friend, madly digging and packing as much as our small cars could carry. As hard as we worked, we barely made a dent in the removal. The following weekend, we expanded to three diggers and two trucks. When both trucks were jammed full, we all stood back in amazement. Despite the removal of a huge quantity of plants, the donor garden looked untouched.

In a few hours, we had thinned out established beds, cleared an old nursery bed, and made way for a new path. There was still an enormous amount left to do—and take—but part of the wisdom of acquisition is knowing when to stop. The first week's haul had half-filled my little nursery bed. The second's packed it to the bursting point, turning it into a garden show display, spilling over with riches. It looked rather fetching, but like those pretty but ephemeral displays, such a state of affairs can't last.

When you get a sudden influx of plants, the first step is to stabilize them someplace, whether in a temporary bed or in pots. The next step is to figure out where all the new plants are going to go. If you are lucky enough to have a friend present you with such a haul in the spring, you are doubly in luck. Spring is an excellent time to move dormant trees, shrubs, and perennials, which will wake up happily in their new homes. Even lots of early bloomers like lungworts (*Pulmonaria* species) that are already showing color can be moved with impunity, so long as you take them with a generous rootball.

Giving and receiving plants

How to move a plant

In my case, placement of these newcomers was slightly complicated. Some of the new plants were to be tucked into beds and borders in the new garden. These I quickly heeled in, covering their roots deeply with compost until I could properly plant them. Many plants can sit like this for several weeks without harm. However, if left too long, heeled-in plants can become distorted. They don't stop growing, and if angled oddly or packed too close together, the new growth faithfully reflects their difficulties. If you aren't sure how soon you can plant them, set nursery plants upright and give them some breathing room.

A few of the new maples and shrubby willows were intended to end up more or less where we plunked them. The temporary nursery bed was slated to become an ornamental one that spring, and several plants that made themselves look at home right away remained there. Such chance nursery bed juxtapositions often lead to long-term garden relationships, so keep your eyes open when moving plants about. It's worth remembering, however, that accidental combinations may look terrific yet prove impractical. Sometimes one member is a baby that will soon outgrow its partner in scale, or their cultural needs may be too diverse to permit an ongoing partnership.

For instance, my nursery bed holds a striking golden Mexican orange, *Choisya ternata* 'Sundance', nestled in front of red-twigged dogwoods. It looks great, but the Mexican orange requires sun and good drainage, while the dogwood looks best in moist shade. Still, such ideas can spark others. A red-barked shrubby willow, *Salix alba brizensis* 'Ember Glow', would look dazzling behind the Mexican orange in a sunny spot. Both the ruddy dogwood and a cheerful golden *Aucuba japonica* could enjoy dampish shade.

Other of the new plants were bound for the not-yet-made gardens that will surround the not-yet-made garden school in my yard. These needed more than heeling in in a temporary bed. Indeed, we spent many a following weekend potting up plants in suitable containers, getting them ready to wait through what turned out to be a wacky summer. A long cold spring held everything back until July, when sudden heat made them surge into flower. Lank and floppy, they had to be rearranged in their holding area so that they didn't smother their fellows-in-waiting. It all seems like a lot of trouble, but taking the trouble is what separates gardeners from plant havers.

In short, when we are the recipient of garden generosity, our primary and immediate obligation is to the plants. When kindly people give us plants, it is considered bad form to (a) leave the plants behind when we go home, (b) leave them in the trunk of our car for six months, or (c) take the plants home and let them languish unplanted. All of the above are Not Done in polite plant circles. Or if they are done, they are not done in the face of the giver, who may understandably be miffed.

And what obligation do we have to the giver? Naturally, after such generosity, we open our gardens in return. Not only are off-spring of the gift plants endlessly available to the original giver, should those mother plants ever be lost, but so, too, are any other divisible or spare plants. That direct reciprocity is probably obvious, but the deeper levels of garden giving are not so easy to see. What it involves, as the late Kevin Nicolay was fond of pointing out, is not simply making a certain kind of garden — an avant one that forwards horticulture in some way. It also involves being a certain kind of gardener, one who keeps on giving. That's the real lesson here.

Making Mail Order Work

April

As the April rain streams relentlessly down, my porch
fills up with packages of plants waiting for a home. Catalog
orders placed during the long winter arrive daily. Fresh from
cozy cold frame or coddled greenhouse, the plants are eager
to get growing. Since all I can offer them is a very soggy bed
in a still-chilly garden, I make them wait a little longer.

Some don't mind much. Plants that arrive in pots of
almost any kind are usually content to remain there until
better accommodations can be made. The obvious exceptions are plants that arrived upside down or inside out —
these benefit from being repotted instantly. It can be very
annoying to open a long-awaited box and discover that your
precious plants are standing on their ears. At best, they are
battered but intact. At worst, they are in expensive fragments. A few years back, when Thompson & Morgan began
shipping plants and bulbs, I spent a fortune on a rare fritil-
lary. The big bulb arrived in a plain manila envelope, without
so much as a piece of paper for padding. Needless to say, the
bulb was too damaged to plant. I returned it and asked for a
replacement, explaining the problem. When the replacement
arrived, it too was packed in the same thin envelope. It took
three tries to get a properly packaged, undamaged bulb. I

finally did get something worth planting, but it required a lot of phone calling and letter writing. By the next year, their system was in better shape and my entire order was fine the first time. Well, almost—as always, lots of what I wanted had already sold out. That, however, is another story.

I know I'm not alone in receiving battered plants, because others report similar problems. I appreciate this, because when lots of people complain that they are consistently getting dried out or inadequately rooted plants from certain sources, I won't recommend those places. Usually, I'll also pass on copies of the complaints to the nursery in question so that they can take care of the difficulties.

Not everybody has the time or patience to see that mail order mistakes get rectified. Sometimes, sadly, it takes some clout to make things happen as they should. That's what the Better Business Bureau is for, and gardeners who experience difficulties with mail order suppliers (or any others) should report the entire sequence of events so that correction can be encouraged officially. Fortunately, this situation is becoming less common with each passing season. As mail order gains in popularity, the nurseries are constantly improving their packing skills. Most nurseries try very hard to make your mail order experience a positive one. In fact, the smaller the company, the more personal the service tends to be. Big companies have a lot at stake as well, and again, most work hard to ensure consumer satisfaction (not always an easy thing to accomplish).

Receiving plants through the mail

However, certain exceptions to this rule don't seem to care much what happens to plants once they leave the nursery. This cavalier attitude can make plant shopping by mail a frustrating experience. If you receive a package of plants in less than terrific condition, there are several constructive ways to deal with the situation.

First, try to determine where the fault lies. Were the plants undersized, packed with dry roots, inadequately wrapped, or improperly packaged? If so, the problem originates at the nursery. Some people are hesitant to complain about poor packing, especially if the plants survive. They may feel that the nursery people are too busy to bother, or that it doesn't really matter because the plants are more or less okay. Sometimes they just don't want to seem like fusspots.

However, from the nursery's point of view, complaints are really kinder. If you are in business, you want to know if there are problems. Packing problems in particular are very fixable, and most nursery owners will be glad you told them. They won't be delighted to hear that your order was damaged, but it is definitely in everybody's best interest to set things straight.

Most nurseries will do everything possible to make good on your order. With a reputable nursery, packing problems usually occur during emergencies; some key staff person is sick and inexperienced people are filling in for a day, or the temporary spring rush helpers aren't fully trained. Despite good instructions, nongardeners may simply not understand the importance of what they are doing.

Experienced nursery folks not only care about your business, they care about the plants themselves and want good lives for them. Therefore, if the replacement package arrives in similar condition, get the message. Report the matter to both the nursery and the Better Business Bureau, and next time order from somebody else.

If the packing box itself was demolished, the problem lies with the carrier. In this case, both the carrier and the originating nursery should be notified. The carrier should make good on the plants, usually working through the nursery. In any case, the nursery needs to know about the problem. If enough customers have difficulties of that kind, the nursery will very likely change mailing companies.

Even the best nurseries can have bad days or bad luck. If you get a problem-ridden shipment from a nursery you have had consistently good results with in the past, let them know, but give them another chance. If the company is new to you, ask around and see whether other gardeners have had similar or better results before making an order.

Indeed, before I risk a lot of money on an unfamiliar company, I start small, making a modest initial order. If the plants are good sized and fine quality, I'll go ahead and order more next time. On occasion, my initial order is of stupendous quality and loaded with exciting extras. This is, of course, great, but to check for symptoms of celebrity syndrome, I reorder anonymously through several friends. If they, too, receive exceptional stuff, I'll tell everybody about this great find.

If, on the other hand, the friends' orders are markedly less wonderful, I proceed with some suspicion. While it's nice to find a nursery that appreciates my work and sends me extra-wonderful plants, I need to know whether you, too, can expect special treatment. If so, I can warmly and loudly recommend that nursery in a highly public manner. When I do, you can count on your order getting the same quality and care as mine.

Finding a reliable and well-run nursery that supplies both old favorites and new finds is an important part of avant gardening. It involves the same kind of search process as seeking a great dentist or therapist. Some tips come by word of mouth, others come from reading about them or seeing ads promoting something you've been wanting a source for. In England, where garden magazines are as numerous as sex magazines are over here, I once read a fascinating series in a magazine written for professional gardeners. Each week, the staff anonymously ordered the exact same list of plants from about six sources. When they arrived, the plants were photographed to show how they were packed. They were then unwrapped and photographed again to show their initial condition. Finally, the plants were washed clean of soil and the root systems were spread out and photographed one last time. The series was a huge hit with gardeners, but less popular with some nurseries, who felt that random samples were unfair. To make sure things really were fair, any nursery that complained would be included in another trial at a later date, again anonymously, so they could have a chance to redeem themselves. (Some of the plant samples were pretty sad.)

Such tests are, of course, enormously revealing of the quality of plants stocked by various nurseries. It would be a great way to evaluate the overall value, dollar for dollar, of any nurseries you were thinking of patronizing. As a home test, it might be too expensive for most people, unless you were planning to order multiples of certain plants anyway. In that case, you could divide your order among three or five or whatever number of nurseries would make your order come out right. Even if you decided not to rinse the roots of each plant, there would surely be some overall differences that would help to steer future plant purchasing decisions. It would also be a wonderful way for a plant society with regular meetings to evaluate possible plant sources as a group. Keeping a photographic record would help to make comparisons among nurseries over time, as would recording the prices and time it took to receive the orders. If nothing else, it would help to pass the time while waiting for the garden to dry out enough that we can go out and get all those new plants in the ground.

MAY

Sorting Scilla

May

Most older gardens are bright in May. Those sky blue spikes that used to be called *Scilla hispanica* are now known (in some circles, anyway) as *Endymion hispanicus*, or even the Spanish bluebell. A prolific seeder, Spanish bluebell reproduces itself happily when left undisturbed. It also reproduces happily when it *is* disturbed. Try to get rid of it and you learn just how persistent a plant can be. One friend who inherited a large, long-neglected garden has been steadily removing the scilla for close to ten years. Each spring, she digs them out of the long borders and tosses them into the woods, where they plant themselves in the leafy compost. After all this time, and countless scilla removal sessions that include screening the soil to get all the little bulblets out, her borders are still filmed with blue each May.

So, too, are the woods, and that's a far better spot for these determined bulbs. Pretty as they are, they have too much drive to function long term in a border, however mixed of company. Like many a wanderer, scilla puts itself wherever it wants to be regardless of whether that spot has already been allotted to somebody else. It has an annoying habit of choosing the best plants to elbow in on, too. Spend an autumn afternoon preparing a perfect planting hole for a tree peony or a trillium, and next May you will find a bright-eyed bunch of blazingly blue scilla. Look hard and you will also see your struggling tree peony peering out disconsolately from under those lush, strappy leaves. You of course sail in to remove the offender, which you are absolutely positive was not there last fall, and discover that removal is a tricky operation, since the infiltrator has multiplied while you ran to get the trowel.

Actually, though bluebells can be a pest in a formal border, there's no reason to rid the garden of them entirely. The one- to two-foot stalks have an artless charm that accords well with native foam flower (*Tiarella trifolia*) and filmy star flower (*Trientalis latifolia*) in woodsy gardens, or with oxeye daisies in open meadows, or with golden buttercups in damp spots. The blue ones look best in sunny spots, but there are other choices; Spanish bluebells can be clear blue or deeper lake blue as well as pink (really a soft lilac) or white. Indeed, all of these variations are likely to appear in your yard over time.

Cheerful and willing, these adaptable plants bloom their hearts out with no encouragement at all. In my tiny Seattle garden, they bloomed away along the alley, bravely ignoring the onslaughts of motorcycles, tomcats, pooping dogs, and delivery trucks. I collected all the soft pinky ones and set them under an old lilac, whose blossom was just a shade darker. The effect was extremely pretty and turned an ugly patch of alley into something worth looking at. An elderly neighbor gave me starts of sweet woodruff (*Galium odoratum*), which threaded its way between the bulbs in a sheet of scented white stars. That looked so nice that I repeated it at the other end of the alley, where an old bay laurel leaned through my little picket fence. There, I grouped the dark bluebells, which gleamed beautifully against the dark, lustrous laurel leaves and the foamy white woodruff.

Those Seattle scilla came with the garden, but I saw them growing up and down alleys and in vacant lots all over the city. Indeed, scilla have naturalized in parts of the Northwest, making themselves at home wherever they can, even in gardens where their presence was not invited. These plump bulbs are not thugs so much as travelers.

Spread both by seed and by tiny bulblets that remain in the soil when the mother bulb is removed, they pop up in compost heaps and borders with equal abandon. When they insert themselves into the heart of expensive perennials, or spoil a formal planting with their unstudied artlessness, gardeners tend to yank and toss these interlopers without ceremony. However, such adaptable plants can instead be put to excellent use.

Closely related to the English bluebell that hazes woodland and shrubbery with blue each spring, Spanish bluebells will work the same magic for Northwestern gardens. Where they punctuate the lawn or interrupt the bedding out, dig them out with just a bit more care and replace them where they can run and spread to advantage. One of the best places to put them in newer, wooded gardens is over the septic field. It's common practice to "park out" the woods by clearing away underbrush before excavating a drain field. When the soil is replaced, you can weave a tapestry of new understory plants, combining native Oregon grape (*Mahonia* species), evergreen huckleberries, sword ferns, and salal with imported azaleas and rhododendrons. This will create an airy understory that looks far handsomer than barren, artificially empty woods carpeted with turf grass. Snuggle those wandering bluebells between the shrubs, and in a single season they will spread like soft blue smoke over the forest floor. Add some sweet woodruff and let it pour

Spanish
bluebells

in solid sheets under your trees. The bulbs won't mind a bit, and native shrubs like salal and mahonia can penetrate its airy cover without difficulty. I know another island garden where for years every bluebell was patiently transplanted from garden to woods, and they now make a magic carpet beneath huckleberries in the high shade.

In sunnier gardens, you can create bluebell meadows. Pick an area you don't want to mow, and pack it with cast-off bulbs. If your yard doesn't offer enough, put up a note at the library or grocery store. Offer to dig unwanted scilla and you'll be flooded with offers. To avoid an artificial look, and to get the prettiest effect from your bulbs, group them loosely in a few places and let them spread themselves, which they will do in short order. Add some starts of sturdy wildflowers, like blue chicory, Queen Anne's lace, and even the wild sweet pea, whose cheerful, rosy flowers brighten the green all summer. The bluebells will grow everywhere between them, and in the first few years, before the wild things grow up, they will make a blue carpet studded with gold and white.

To make your own meadow or woodland glade, on whatever scale, start in May. It's fine to move bluebells in flower; indeed, it's the only way to tell what color they are. Like many bulbs, they move well in the green (when the foliage is still in strong growth). Group your scilla by color, making sweeps of blue, putting pinks under lilacs or pink and purple brooms like 'Minstead', and matching whites with yellow azaleas or pale pink rhododendrons.

You can put scilla almost anywhere you like and they will adapt quickly to their new home. They don't like standing water but tolerate damp soil in spring so long as the ground dries out enough that their summer dormancy is undisturbed. They do, however, manage to survive just fine where beds are regularly watered in summer. However, newly planted bulbs are more vulnerable to rots than established or even self-sown ones, so don't water them that first summer after planting. Woodland settings are ideal, but even a small shrubbery makes a fine scilla spot too. In meadows, the rising wildflowers hide the scilla foliage as it fades. In shade, mix in some ferns and hostas to cover the gaps left by their lanky foliage as it browns off in June and July.

To move scilla from the garden, dig up the whole clumps with a garden fork, trying not to spear them through the heart. (They are adaptable, but not *that* adaptable.) Shake off any loose soil, then reset the bulbs a few inches apart, shaping them in loose ribbons and clusters. The bulbs will soon fill in the gaps for you, but in the meantime starbursts and clusters will look better than straight lines. You can toss the bulbs about to get a natural look, or better yet, have the kids plant them for a truly random effect. For the price of an afternoon's work, next spring and for years to come, you will enjoy your own magical bluebell wood.

Packing Pots for Smashing Shows

May

Most years, by May warmer weather has arrived, allowing us to start setting out annuals. When we get a prolonged, cool spring, people wonder, "How come my petunias are shrinking?" and "Why is my basil turning brown?" In both cases, the answer is the same: because tropical plants don't enjoy southern Alaska. There's no way to provide a hard-and-fast date for putting out annuals. Some years, April comes in warm and leaves warmer. When that happens, you can set anything out early and it won't be retarded by a sudden cold snap. However, other years are the yo-yo kind, when temperatures fluctuate fast and often.

Yo-yo years don't slow down the tough old standbys like sweet alyssum or calendulas, but they can really discourage tender tropicals like nicotiana, petunias, and zinnias. May is often the transition month between spring and summer, and even in a mild year, it's not uncommon to experience cool nights (in the 40s and 50s) right into June. When that happens, we need to protect hothouse prima donnas to keep them from losing their luster. By the time more consistent heat finally arrives in earnest, usually around mid May, we're no longer worrying about providing snow suits for the little monkeys. Instead, we need to consider offering some sunblock for the newly planted, especially in a swing year when wildly changing temperatures make hardening off a challenge. Since face cream would probably clog their little pores, screening is a better way to go.

For individual plants, you can use small pieces of cheesecloth or remay (a light, woven plant cover cloth that baffles bugs as well as sun) to block plants from full sun. This makes the garden look like the aftermath of a stylish picnic (the kind where people use napkins) for a few days, it's true. The payoff, however, is that your investment doesn't crisp up before you get to enjoy it. Where several new plants are grouped, a window screen can be propped to create filtered shade for a day or two. This also gives the garden an interesting appearance (my mother would probably call it "the Okie look"), but hey, we can't make omelets without getting a few broken eggshells, right?

Newly purchased plants that got their start in greenhouses are not always hardened off enough to face real life without a little help from us. Cool weather can stunt their growth as surely as smoking, but a sudden influx of really hot weather can also give plants trouble. Usually it's not the heat so much as the direct sunlight that does the damage. Shade, whether contrived or natural, gives tender new arrivals a chance to adjust to the more robust atmosphere of the open garden. It may feel odd to tuck sunflowers and roses in the shade, but even confirmed sun lovers will benefit from a few days' respite before facing up to their new reality.

Container plantings may also qualify for the shade treatment. It's not necessary when you are transferring a large, outdoor-grown plant to a pot. Plants that are already adjusted to sun and wind won't mind moving (unless you move them on a very hot day). Little plants, however, may well show some stress if they are whisked into dazzling prominence. This is especially true with the popular liners and plugs sold for cramming into showy pots. One weekend, for instance, I spent a happy hour plundering Johnson's Nursery (on Bainbridge Island), where tiny plugs can run as little as 15 cents and most big ones are under a quarter. Faced with such abundance and variety, the temptation to load up on old favorites is simply irresistible.

I came home with an armload of pot-ables, from spicy 'Lemon Gem' marigolds and blue basil to copper-leaved fuchsias with tawny, tubular flowers ('Gartenmeister') and dusky-leaved begonias with huge, smoldering red flowers of utterly satisfying vulgarity.

Back home, each large pot was given a centerpiece, perhaps a white Chilean potato vine (*Solanum jasminoides*) or a crinkly, black-leaved begonia with salmon blossoms (these are marginally more tasteful than the red ones but equally showy). Next came secondary plants like arching *Scaevola aemula* 'Blue Wonder', whose starry little blue flowers never quit, or bundles of fragrant purple heliotrope with quilted black leaves. Each pot was then encircled with a spiller to soften the pot lip. Upright fuchsias got skirts of golden deadnettle (*Lamium maculatum* 'Aureum'), which will cascade in sunny tumbles within a month. Softer compositions got stiffer sprays of fuzzy *Helichrysum petiolare* in celadon, sage-and-gray, or lemon lime.

We also made a series of hanging baskets, using dangling begonias and compact coleus in wonderful patterns for the shady porch and fuchsias and geraniums for the sunny side. My all-time favorite fuchsia is a trailer called 'Autumnale', whose long arms are hung with large, copper and bronze leaves that are streaked with red and old gold. The small flowers are pinky purple and look like holiday tree ornaments. Next to it hangs a huge basket of *Fuchsia* 'Island Sunset', another drooper with rose and gold leaves all streaked with slate and sand. It is partnered with an oddball ivy-leaf geranium called 'Crocodile', whose thick, almost succulent leaves are curiously veined in yellow and really do resemble crocodile skin.

Screening plants

Planting showy pots

Once planted, all these creations got a long drink of warm water. Not bath water, mind you, but wrist temperature stuff. (Cold water can shock a young tropical as much as a cold night.) I also mixed a handful of time-release fertilizer into each container, scratching it lightly into the top inch or so of soil. It's worth remembering that nearly all of these pelletized feeds can't release their nutrients until soil temperatures reach about 75 degrees, which may take quite a while in the garden.

Pots and containers, however, are usually a good deal warmer, so those nutrients are available almost at once. Because pots, baskets, and containers are watered so often, they are usually leached of soil nutrients within the first month or so. If we want them to keep perking along, we need to provide an ongoing source of dinner. If you prefer, you can water with a soluble fertilizer every week or so, but it is far simpler to use these little vitamins (Osmacote is perhaps the best known), especially when you will be gone on vacation, with others doing the watering for you. The last step for my potted delights was to give them a shady place to regroup for a few days. Only after signs of new growth occurred did they finally take their place in the sun.

Creating Color Themes

 May

I am often asked how I come up with color themes and how they are developed. I am slightly embarrassed to admit that many of my most satisfying combinations begin by accident and evolve through greed. Color work can, of course, be planned, and sometimes is, but usually I am working with whatever is at hand, which is generally a very mixed bag. For smitten gardeners, plants are impulse items; we see, we are conquered, we buy. This is an excellent way to accumulate creative material, but spontaneous buying sprees can lead to disappointments when we get our loot back home. Plants that looked magnificent when surrounded by four hundred cousins may look lonely on their own. Colors that thrilled us at the nursery can look out of place in our own backyards. What's a plant addict to do?

The first problem has a simple solution: Buy more. Lots more. Then, before committing them to the ground, place the newcomers in attractive clusters so they catch and hold the eye. A quick experiment will demonstrate how this works. Set a single primrose in a garden bed; nothing much happens. Now set out a cluster of similarly colored primroses; together, they show up nicely. The same holds true for most perennials, especially if the individual plants never get very large.

This concept is the basis for a cardinal principle of good garden making: Abundance is Good. Of course, once this point becomes clear, it is easy to get carried away. Garden books are always urging us to plant in big sweeps, but unless you live on an enormous estate, one good sweep (or a sweep of one) might be all you have room for. The key here is moderate abundance, because while too much of anything can be boring, too little often looks insignificant. Finding the balance between variety and a comforting repetition requires us to try several scenarios out before choosing the one we want to play out right now. This means, once again, that we need enough kinds of plants for variety and enough of each plant for soothing repetition as well as for sufficiently emphatic effect.

Once we have brought home the right raw materials in the right quantities, how can we use them to greatest advantage? That graceful sweep can be tricky to achieve, and what is more commonly seen could more truthfully be characterized as lumps and blobs. Instead of planting in color blocks, try thinking in terms of those wandering ribbons of birds, which frequently alter in width. Rather than making a wobbly line that wiggles through the border but remains three plants wide, try creating clusters and colonies, with outlying satellites of smaller amounts. This direct application of chaos theory works even on a tiny scale, with alpine plants in a miniature rockery. In the border, it means interweaving several kinds of plants at each end of what was formerly a solid block of one kind. If you are working remedially, try loosening up the edges of each color block, combining a few outlying plants with their neighbors to blur those abrupt territorial perimeters.

To do this from the get-go, try arranging plants in little bursts and drifts before planting them. Since odd-numbered groups look more natural, experiment with groups of three or five or seven plants. Repeat such groups several times and the effect is amplified delightfully. Yes, you are right; this requires lots of plants. Those of us on tight budgets are well served by learning good propagation skills, since many perennials are quite easy to increase by division. Buy one plant, set it in a nursery bed, treat it well, and within a year or two, you can pull that original single plant to pieces to get a dozen or more offspring. Also, when kind friends offer you seedlings and divisions from their own gardens, ask for plants that there are lots of. Good growers make good starter plants for novice colorists (or anybody), and it's easier to be really generous with their placement than when we are dealing with finicky and expensive darlings that increase grudgingly. It can indeed be a statement to have a huge row of, say, the legendary black bugbane, *Cimicifuga ramosa* 'Brunette', but it may read more like a bank statement than a colorist commentary. The idea is to start experiment-

Arranging color schemes in the garden

ing by using willing and available plants in quantity, the rarities sparingly and placed for maximum impact. As anywhere else in life, thoughtful generosity pays a big dividend in the garden. We do not, however, need to bust our budgets to create a satisfying and last-ingly beautiful display.

Another common query concerns combining colors without creating war or a visual jumble. The solution to color clashes and incompatibilities is to choose a theme and stick with it. You can still bring home plants that catch your fancy, but try limiting your choices to cool pastels or hot sunset colors. To simplify even further, consider buying only plants with blue (or yellow, or white) flowers or leaves. You can also expand your theme by combining shades of blue with whites and yellows (or any colors that you like together). Avoidance also works: Margaret Ward, a garden doyenne of my acquaintance, built her fabulously colorful garden on Bainbridge Island over many decades. Her admirable goal was to have some-thing in color and good looks all year long. In a small space, this can be a challenge, but she rose to it marvelously. She did it in part by shopping all year long, always seeking out off-season performers that would appreciate her seaside conditions. In color terms, her mandate was very simple: She simply refused ground space to any-thing pink. This kind of reverse color editing allowed her to spin harmonious runs that are spirited yet never clash.

As we mature as gardeners, we often find that our taste is changing too. If your whole garden has been a pastel dreamland for years, yet you find yourself bringing home exotic beauties in sizzling reds and purples, it might be time to branch out a bit. This doesn't mean you have to scrap your old garden favorites (at least, not all at once or right away). An infusion of warmer, brighter shades and tints of your chosen colors can often add vigor to a demure, retiring pastel color scheme. Try seeking out ashen pastels (those shaded with black) and some clearer tints of the same hues. Mingled with the softer tones already in place, the darker ones will add depth to your palette, while the lighter, brighter ones bring clarity and snap. If this gradual approach works for you, your new treasures can simply slip in amongst your old favorites.

Sometimes, however, more brazen newcomers just don't mingle sedately amongst your prim pinks and proper lavenders. In that case, the solution is once again to buy more plants, in colors and forms that complement these oddballs. To create a new bed to accommodate your developing color theme, just slice up another chunk of lawn (composted grass turves make great new soil), dig in some compost and aged manure, and plant away. It's helpful to remember that gardens are really very fluid. Adventurous gardeners prove this all the time, for in their yards, beds come and go, shifting contents and position at the gardener's whim. Grass is not sacred, and it is quite easy to dig out. The earth's green skin can be lifted and recovered with a richer variety of plants, and in the process our lives may be greatly enriched as well. If only all problems could be so pleasantly solved!

Garden Basics

May

Every spring, I receive a spate of questions about garden basics. How do you divide plants? Do different kinds of plants get split up differently? Why do my seedlings turn fuzzy and die?

Some of these topics—like seedling care—are covered clearly in so many garden books that it would be repetitious to repeat it all in great depth. However, in short, seeds need (1) a nutritious medium to grow in, (2) water, (3) light, and (4) air. It used to be hard to find decent potting soil blends, and most serious gardeners made their own. These days, really good commercial soil mixes are widely available. I have been very pleased with the Whitney Farms organic potting soils and now use them rather than fuss with home-made mixes. If the seed you are sowing is very fine, you can lighten the mix by adding either a little more sand to increase drainage or vermiculite, which holds extra water for plants like hellebores that appreciate the moisture. Pack the mix into your seed trays (or pots or pie tins or whatever you are using) firmly, then scatter on the seed. Some seeds need light to germinate, and if so, it will say so on the packet.

As for sowing seed, there's nothing like following directions. Most seed packets are quite clear about how to space the seed and how deep to cover it (if at all). Watching my kids grow all kinds of things with amazing results, I have come to think that simple faith and natural exuberance are more important than sterile technique. To moisten the seed trays, I prefer a spray bottle over watering cans. For one thing, the watering cans with fine roses (those metal add-ons that reduce the water volume) clog at the slightest provocation. Rather than buy fancy bottled water for my plants, I use an old spray bottle once (literally) used when ironing clothes. It works fine with ordinary tap water, and since I haven't ironed for years, it's a fitting piece of practical recycling.

To keep seed trays from drying out, I cover them with muslin or cheesecloth, which I dampen with the same spray bottle. This light covering also shelters seedlings from excess sun, should there ever be any. When the seedlings are big enough to push the cover up, they are big enough to want more sun. If you have had trouble with damping off (that's when the baby plants get fuzzy and die), try using fresh bags of sterilized soil mix, and don't cover the seedlings. More air and clean soil should take care of that particular demon. In her delightful book, *A Country Garden* (now out of print, but well worth seeking out at used bookstores), Josephine Nuese talks about giving seedlings more air by punching holes in the sides of her seed trays (she favored aluminum pie tins, like many of her generation). It's true that many seedlings appreciate extra air at the roots and will often grow especially well in ventilated containers. Don't grow seedlings in a draft, but do put them where they get free passage of air, rather than in some dim basement with no air circulation.

Light, if you recall, is another issue. Seeds often germinate in the dark—indeed, some need to—but a few require full light to germinate and don't want even a light covering of soil. Again, your seed packet will make these predilections clear. Most seedlings don't much care about light until they sprout, at which point they want quite a bit of it. Indoors, I have had the best success growing seeds under grow lights that can be raised or lowered as needed. Out-of-doors, seedlings grown in cold frames have done fine with ordinary daylight.

What rarely works is the old sunny windowsill. For one thing, our sun is not very reliable early in the year (or at any other time, really). For another, it's often quite cold outside. By the time we push our leaning little seedlings close enough to the light, they are getting chilblains. It's also not good for seedlings to expend so much energy following the light. They develop a huge tilt when placed too far from their light source, so we turn their pots. Next day, they reverse the tilt with all their might. If the light source is directly overhead and well placed, neither too close nor too far away, the little guys can concentrate on becoming whole plants. Those early childhood traumas linger on in plants as well as people, so start them right and try to avoid such warping experiences.

Once the first true leaves appear, seedlings can be potted up into two- or four-inch pots, depending on their eventual size. From there, they go on into larger pots or straight into the garden. Plants that have grown up inside must be hardened off before facing the big outdoors permanently. This also applies to newly purchased plants that were raised in greenhouses. Like seedlings, they will make the transition from cozy to chilly far better if allowed to do it in stages. We all fear change, and our plants are no exception. Take them out for an hour or so the first day, introducing them to gentle light and wind but protecting them from full-on exposure. The next day, leave them out for a couple of hours. Add time each day, and by the end of a week or so, they will be ready to adapt. Obviously, if there is a sudden cold snap or heat wave, you will need to cut back their outdoor time until the weather settles down again.

Seedling care

Dividing perennials

Good information on how to divide perennials is harder to come by than seed talk. If most books present such information more sketchily, it's because the topic is too complex to be dealt with in a few paragraphs. Also, authors rarely go into specific detail about plant division because it is essentially an intuitive process. Experienced gardeners will usually say that the plants tell them how they want to be divided, or that their hands "just kind of know what to do," or something along those lines. Such unscientific terms come off as anthropomorphic babble to true techies, who love clear and specific instructions. Loose chat about touchy-feely interspecies communication leaves such folks feeling frustrated and skeptical. I can understand that, yet it happens to be true.

There are, however, a few useful rules that lump plants by basic root structures and types. For instance, plants like hostas, daylilies, and Siberian iris have thick storage roots that make what needs doing fairly obvious. Dig up last year's new hosta and you will see that masses of tightly clustered crowns are crammed together. It looks like a single entity, but if the mom plant is gently wiggled and jiggled, the apparent lump will come apart pretty easily into discrete plants, each with its own set of roots. Just pull those rooted crowns loose, reset them in refreshed soil, and there you are.

This works great for smallish plants that don't actually *need* division but are large enough to split. With heftier, more mature plants, far more force may be necessary. Densely crammed crowns of big mamma daylilies must be boldly ripped apart. Teasing won't get you anywhere, but a machete will cut to the core of things. Make one big whack across the center of the stubborn plant, and the rest will fall into place. Usually, older plants that are too big to split by hand will have a tough central core that is too woody to be productive anyway. Toss the oldest bits into the compost, divide the remainder into as many plants as you like, and reset them where you want lots.

Some plants require active assistance from another person just to get them out of the ground. Big pampas grasses or maiden grasses most certainly fall into this category. Find a friend who wants some, get two garden forks, and start digging in from each side. Loosen the soil all the way around the rootball, then rock that puppy back and forth until it breaks loose. If it won't, slide a shovel in underneath the rootball and slice the last roots. Smaller people may want to slip a tarp under the rootball during the rocking process. They can then lift the plant with the tarp, which is usually easier than trying to tug a bulky, heavy rootball out of a hole. Once you have the beast free, get it to a good working surface. I perform surgery on the lawn, but turf worshipers will heartily disapprove of this idea. If the lawn is the best spot but must be protected, you can put down a sheet of plywood for a work surface. In any case, once you have the plant where you can work on it, size it up and decide how you want to approach the next stage.

Most big grasses make such solid lumps that you need a hatchet or machete to whack them into smaller chunks. Before you do, it is advisable to cut back the long strands of grass that will otherwise flop in your face. Indeed, with many grasses, you may want to give them a quick haircut before digging them out. Lots of grasses have enough silica in their blades to make them effective cutting tools. It's bad enough getting sliced across the arm or hand, but a stem poke or grass cut in an eye is no joke. To prevent what can be serious damage, always wear glasses or protective goggles when you divide big grasses (or even weed around them). Once armed and protected, you can attack the division problem. I like to use a heavy wood maul to split large grass clumps, but I know people who swear by wood saws. Axes are classic grass division tools, but experiment and you may find something that suits you better. As with many plants, big grasses may have less vigorous roots at their cores. Discard any chunks that don't look frisky, and reduce the rest to the size you want to replant. Although this process can be attempted in almost any season, spring division of grasses is least risky in terms of plant recovery and losses.

Most garden perennials can be divided in spring or fall, and here the rule of thumb is to divide early bloomers late and late bloomers early. Summer bloomers divided in spring will bloom late or not at all that first year, but otherwise the timing is a matter of convenience. Ardent runners like mint, and many ground covers can be pulled to pieces and reset without much finesse almost anytime. It's pretty hard to kill these plants, so nearly anything you do to relieve their congestion will be rewarded.

Certain plants, however, like bleeding hearts (*Dicentra*), are fragile. Their delicate root systems would just as soon shatter as look at you. These need planting with care, and division is a bit tricky until you know their ways. Here, incautious experiment is apt to leave you plantless. When working with an unfamiliar plant, consult a good reference book first. My standby is Margery Fish, a postwar

English garden writer who combines a breezy style and utter practicality with tremendous knowledge. I have a full set of her books (most are now out of print but are always turning up in used bookstores), and no matter what I am seeking, she mentions it in one of her works. Other good guides are those by Graham Stuart Thomas, Beth Chatto, and Christopher Lloyd (who is most practical and detailed in his earlier books).

The great majority of perennials fall somewhere in between these extremes. To build an experience base, start by experimenting with relatively common plants. Cheap and easily replaced, these are terrific candidates for those first life (or death) lessons. If you lose a few, it's no great loss. It's wise to remind ourselves that we learn most effectively through making mistakes. Better to take risks, win some, lose some, than to stagnate, which is no fun at all.

JUNE

Gardening with
Bambi and the Bobcat

 June

When I began gardening, more years ago than I care to admit, my plot was in a quiet New England town where the local fauna consisted of cats, dogs, and kids. Since then, I have had gardens in Ohio and Denver, at ten thousand feet elevation in the Rockies, in several cities and quite a few suburbs, and on a rural farm. Until now, however, I have never really gardened. All that past experience pales beside the whole new world of interactive gardening now opening up for me. No, it's not about the Internet (though my kids keep telling me to come on in, the virtual water's fine). This is the real thing at last: gardening in my own backyard with Bambi and the bobcat.

A few nights ago they staged a demonstration of the prey-predator relationship that makes coyote urine such an effective deer repellent. Late one night, our housecats began subvocalizing in an unearthly chorus. Outside the door, somebody joined them, yowling and growling in a way that prickled the back of my neck. It was too dark to see more than a large, slinky, catlike creature bounding away, but despite certain people's skepticism, I remain convinced it was the local bobcat. The next morning, Bambi and friends arrived as usual at coffee time. They nibbled a few roses, then browsed their way up the hillside. When they got to my pots in the front garden, the whole crew took one sniff and bounded away themselves in what appeared to be panic.

Now, it isn't always easy (or convenient) to have a large predatory animal in the garden, nor are they always so obliging as to leave their markers where you want them. However, an enterprising family in Maine has made it possible for gardeners to use predator urines to direct the flow of animals into or out of our gardens. To learn more about this astonishing concept, I called Ken Johnson, president of Johnson & Company Wilderness Products, most of which are liquid animal excreta.

I already knew that coyote urine was a hot horticultural commodity among local gardeners. It turns out that bobcat and fox urines are equally in demand and for similar reasons. When deer, rabbits, or other browsers smell the scent of their predators, Johnson explains, they avoid the marked area. In the garden, this means placing urine-soaked objects six to eight feet apart around the perimeter of the area to be protected. Some people soak sponges, while others use feminine hygiene items (yuck).

Bainbridge Gardens, a wonderful local nursery with a rich heritage, has developed a unique, effective, and discreet way to use these odoriferous substances. "With most of the dispensers, the coyote urine evaporates too fast," notes Chris Harui, co-owner of the nursery. "We put it in floral picks, with a little piece of string for a wick. It works great, and you can hang them or poke them in pots you want to protect." (Floral picks look like little test tubes with rubber stoppers that are sliced so that stems can fit in but water — or whatever — won't slip out.)

What everyone really wants to know is how the stuff gets collected. "Once we train the animals to hit the bottle, it's no problem," Ken Johnson reveals. He went on to say that the five to six thousand gallons that gardeners buy each year amounts to a mere six to seven percent of the family's business. For sheer volume, hunters, nature photographers, and fisherfolk put us to shame. Johnson swears that these people smear themselves with these fascinating substances. "This practice goes back historically to a time when hunting was a matter of survival, not a sport," he claims. "Hunters wanted to smell like something the animal would accept. If they could find deer or fox or raccoon urine in the wild, it would camouflage their human scent, allowing them to sneak up closer. Photographers want to lure animals closer. Gardeners do the same thing in reverse, using the natural instincts of animals to move them around. These urines are triggers to those instincts."

Though we haven't seen the bobcat (or cougar, as several neighbors insist) again, I did buy some coyote urine, and it seems to work. However, although the deer aren't much in evidence, the creatures just keep on coming. A family of wild chickens has been moving slowly up the driveway toward the house. Every day, they come a bit closer, to the disgruntlement of the cats, who remember chickens all too well. These look like descendants of somebody's Silver Wyandots, elegantly patterned birds in tasteful blends of black, white, and gold. They will certainly be an ornament to the garden, most helpful weeders, but death to young seedlings. This sudden influx of creatures makes me think that instead of trying to start a garden, I should take a tip from the Johnson clan down Maine and start my own wild animal farm. Chicken urine, anyone?

Wily ways to keep animals out of the garden

Many area nurseries stock the liquid animal excreta mentioned here. Those who can't find it can call Johnson & Company Wilderness Products toll-free at 800/527-6766 to order some.

Stellar Lupines: The Woodfield Brothers' New Generation

 June

Sixty years ago, the Russell lupines set a new standard for border plants. Bred over a twenty-five-year period by York-shireman George Russell and introduced to the market in 1937, the Russell strain elevated a sometimes weedy species to high horticultural status. Outstanding for plant form and color range, the Russells were the quintessential border lupine for decades. Russell based his strain on our Northwestern native *Lupinus polyphyllus* forms selected in Canada, crossing them with western tree lupine (*Lupinus arboreus*) and a few unrecorded annual species to create color breaks. These hybrids displayed an exciting array of colors, dramatically enlarging the simple palette of the species (blooms of blue, pink, purple, or white in *L. polyphyllus* and yellow, blue, or lavender in *L. arboreus*).

The original Russell strain offered both delicate pastels and shining jewel tones as well as bicolors and tricolors. Pink deepens to rose and pales to chalk. Blue shades to hazy lavender and purple as well as clear sky and water tones. The yellows encompass a huge range of tints, from lemon and cream to copper and orange, buff, and brick. Over time, sadly, this glorious seed strain lost its edge. By the 1950s, George Russell had retired from active horticulture, passing his breeding stock on to Baker's Nursery in Wolverhampton, England. After World War II, the troubled British economy made for reduced nursery staff. Without adequate attention, the strain began to deteriorate badly.

Enter the Brothers Woodfield. Ex-guardsmen turned nursery-men, Brian and Maurice Woodfield had spent decades improving older strains of delphiniums and gladiolus through meticulous rese-lection. When they noticed the degeneration of the once-famed Russells, they were dismayed.

"The Russells were brilliant plants, just remarkable, but it only took a few years of neglect for the line to weaken," says Maurice Woodfield. "If nobody is actively breeding, but just maintaining existing stock, any strain will deteriorate. You could see that hap-pening within two years."

Though the Woodfield Nursery in Stratford-on-Avon is tiny, the brothers found room for the remaining breeding stock and began to repair the damage. "The Canadian plants Russell worked with all had a flattened keel which was folded back on itself, so that you could see right through the flowers," notes Brian Woodfield. "Russell eliminated that by selecting for fuller keels that lay flat, hor-izontal with the bell of the blossom. This made for a fuller, more compact spike and a much better-looking plant."

In reselecting the New Generation series, the Woodfields kept several goals in mind. "We bred for sturdy stems and shorter foliage, so the plants don't need staking under normal garden conditions. This also helps to keep plants from looking so tatty once the blooming is past," Brian explains. "The other big problem we saw was with premature browning. In poor flowers, the blossoms at the base are dying off before the top ones have opened. We wanted show-quality spikes that remained in top form longer, with the whole spike open at once. This prolongs the bloom period somewhat as well."

Russell lupines

New Generation lupines

To this end, the two relentlessly rogued out any plants that didn't have the desired qualities. Vigor, good overall form, and sturdy structure were the main requirements, with bigger, better blossoms running a close second. The gratifying result is a line of compact plants that stand up to wind and weather yet retain the towering three-foot bloom spikes of the original Russell strain.

"It went quite fast, really," Maurice comments. "In just two or three years, we had pretty well eradicated both problems. With a sound breeding program established, we could start working on color breaks, trying to increase the range." This they have done dazzlingly well, offering two dozen named forms as well as mixed color blends.

The Woodfields also wanted to improve several long-standing health problems that plague lupines. "We have almost eliminated mildew in our fields," Maurice points out with justifiable pride. "Give New Generation lupines plenty of water in spring and early summer, and you won't see mildew. That comes from dry roots, and is quite avoidable."

Aphids are still a problem, Brian admits, "particularly the Canadian aphid, which luckily is fairly easy to get rid of." Mild attacks can be controlled with a hose, just by washing the plants off. Insecticidal soaps are useful for larger infestations, as are catchment crops of nasturtiums, which lure aphids away from almost anything.

In the garden, these sturdy turrets are invaluable for bringing bold lines and strong color to the May garden. Plants begin blooming in late spring and carry on into summer. As they fade, cut away the old bloom spikes and you will encourage a smaller crop of secondary blooms. Unlike the weakly older strains, these lupines are good for years, acting like true perennials and not collapsing into ruin in midsummer.

Because the seed strain is still mostly sold as a mixture, it can be difficult to use these lupines well in colorist borders. When you can't tell what color is going to appear, careful mixing and matching become impossible. One solution is to grow the lupines on in pots, sinking them into nursery rows until they reveal their true colors, then placing them in the garden. Another is to seek out seed sources for the single color strains, which are not yet widely available, even in England. Keep your eyes open, though, because these days good plants travel fast, and yesterday's impossible-to-find treasure can turn up at the grocery store nursery area in no time flat.

So far, only one wholesale nursery is growing the New Generation lupines in North America, but your favorite retail nursery can order them for you (if you live in the Pacific Northwest). The wholesale source is Log House Plants, 78185 Rat Creek Road, Cottage Grove, OR 97424. Their order number is 800/564-4115. This is *not* a retail nursery, so please work with your local nursery to place an order. (Log House is also the only source for the improved Pacific Giant delphiniums, which are well worth growing.)

Garden Moving Etiquette

June

In the tumult of moving or preparing for a major move, gardeners spend a lot of time organizing their plants and making plans. Even while packing up dishes or boxes of books, we are wondering constantly where this or that cherished plant should go. It's easy to forget, in the throes of such upheaval, that these are not the only questions to be asking. It is equally important to remember that there is an etiquette to moving a garden. I was constantly reminded of this during the move from the old farmhouse. Prospective buyers were coming through the garden (and the house; some of them actually want to look at the house as well, oddly enough), and many of these folks ask which plants will be left for them.

Now, there are specific legal guidelines for marking plants that will not be left behind. The garden mover must mark everything and anything that will or might go, labeling them clearly so that the buyers understand exactly what they will or won't be getting. However, the freemasonry of gardeners dictates an even more compelling set of guidelines, all the more stringent for being part of our (usually) unspoken code.

Our major goal should be that the garden we are leaving behind look lovely and full for its new owners. The first rule, therefore, is that there must not be big potholes in the borders.

The garden should not look raided, with gaping pits where something fun clearly used to be. Even if the beds are crowded enough
that the gaps will later be hidden, at least fill
those telltale holes with good soil. In my case,
many people were also coming through to
remove and caretake plants. Since there was
too much going on for me to cope with single-
handedly, I asked these people to replace their
own divots. A large pile of compost and another of manure were at
hand, so as each group of plants went to new homes, fresh soil could
be dumped in the holes.

Moving
a garden

The next rule of thumb is that there ought not to be huge gaps
between plants. If you remove something structural and important,
replace it with something else. The nurseries are always full of bargains on staple plants, so it's easy to find suitable, sizable, and reasonably priced substitutes. In older, crowded gardens, you may have
something just right squashed away into a corner that, given more
room, could fill this key role happily. Indeed, it was a source of
wonder to me that so many forgotten plants turned up as we
removed the favorites that blocked them from view. It's also kind of
fun to rearrange things differently, and to remember why you
bought that overlooked beauty in the first place. Creating new patterns with them is kind of like imagining how your own life might
be different if you had partnered with a different person.

To further smooth the transition between owners, divide rather
than remove your plants whenever possible, so that the coherence of
your composition isn't lost. Reset all those divisions in decent soil,
and pot your share up into a mixture of compost and aged manure,
and both sets will be growing strongly within a few weeks. If you
are working against time, you can take chunks off the back of
mother plants and pot them up for your new garden, leaving the
mother plant relatively undisturbed. This method works well in
both spring and fall, though when done late in the season, you will
need to cut back lanky foliage before potting the starts on. As you
work, you can also collect and label ripe seed of clematis,
columbines, poppies, and whatever else you want to have growing

in your next garden. Those little manila envelopes designed for coin storage make excellent seed savers, and a box of five hundred is very inexpensive. I keep a large handful in my tool basket all the time, so I can stuff them with fresh seed as I work. When the seed is freshly collected like that, it is often cluttered up with bits of leaf and stem and whatnot. Rather than sealing the envelopes and creating ideal conditions for mildew, I leave them open, setting them upright into an unsealed zip-close plastic bag so they don't spill. Later, when there is more leisure, you can tumble the packets out on a plate, clean away the chaff, and store the dried seed properly.

It's also thoughtful to prune border shrubs and clematis properly before you leave. This shows the new owners how to handle each plant when it's their turn. Shrub roses, border buddleias, arctic willows, and so forth all have their specific pruning requirements. Indeed, the truly thoughtful gardener will offer to make a garden notebook for the next owners, spelling out such specifics month by month to guide them in caring for the garden.

You can also, of course, root those cuttings for your next garden. Have pots full of sandy loam or compost mixed with grit already prepared before you begin pruning. As you work, you can stick small batches of similar cuttings into each pot. Labels save head-scratching later, when you can't recall exactly which iris or daylily or whatever it was you wanted to save.

Finally, whether you move a lot of plants or just a few, all beds and borders should be tidied and mulched and ready to grow. In the case of serious gardeners, there is a further complication to all this. On the one hand, it is possible that whoever buys our homes won't even want a garden. When I was selling the farm, some people actually wanted to look at the house first and expressed only a vague interest in the garden (I'm not making this up). After such an exchange, I felt fiercely protective toward the wonderful plants that would be left behind. My mind filled with images of giant bulldozers tearing heedlessly through the borders, and I started making feverish and impossible plans to remove everything, including my nice dirt. When we left our Seattle house, the next people built a deck over dirt I had worked on for five years. I loved that dirt; you could plunge your arm in it up to the elbow. Had I known it would be doomed to lie fallow under a deck, I would certainly have hauled it away and replaced it with ordinary fill.

On the other hand, it is possible that whoever buys our gardens (and houses) will actually be wanting these particular gardens, more or less as they are. In my best-case scenario, I envisioned a buyer who genuinely wanted a complex, multilayered garden, one who wouldn't mind the steep learning curve involved in discovering how to care for it over a full year. To this end, I divided plants rather than removing them completely and left certain key things that are quite hard to replace. (They were also—let's be frank—hard to move.)

However, even somebody who wants the kind of garden fanatics make might well be rather overwhelmed by it, so we are wise to simplify them somewhat. In my case, kind friends removed many prima donna plants that demand exacting treatment. We also took out a few irreplaceable heritage plants, including some that were bred or passed on to me by friends who are now gone themselves. All these treasures went to nursery-owning friends who would multiply them properly. Their garden places were filled instead with more ordinary beauties that don't need coddling.

Though taking such steps might seem sad, I was fascinated to notice that instead to me they felt steeped in hopefulness. I knew the garden would go on, changing with its new owners. It will move to its own new life, exactly as it should, and so will I. *Floreat!* Let it all flower.

Angelic Herbs

June

With all the excitement surrounding the new craze for hardy tropicals, one of my favorite plants is edging its way out of the kitchen garden and into the border. Actually, lovers of the large have been growing it in borders for years, for few frankly ornamentals are as statuesque as this unassuming culinary herb. *Angelica archangelica*, the traditional source of candy grass for cake decoration, handily earns a spot in gardens where exotic foliage is wanted.

Grown from seed (which must be fresh to germinate), angelica takes a couple of seasons to arrive at bloom size. These majestic, cutleaf herbs rise to six or eight feet in late spring, when their great flower heads expand, often exceeding dinner plates in size. Studded with small creamy chartreuse flowers, the flower heads are compellingly attractive to bees and wasps, who gather by the score to swill the tasty nectar.

By early summer, mature angelicas are heavy with seed. Their stout, ridged, plum-colored stalks seem so sturdy that it is always a surprise when they come crashing down in wet windstorms. That big foliage acts like a sail, catching enough wind to topple stems as wide as my wrist. The effect can be devastating to neighboring plants, so it is wise to keep your eyes open for the first sign of listing in wet years. The plants usually look terrific right up to the day the rainy winds arrive. It's painful but smart to begin surgery at the first sign of slumping. Placing them in a sheltered position out of the wind helps enormously, so remember that for next time. So, too, does cutting off the great blooms, which not only retards crashing but keeps these ardent reproducers from filling the borders with scores of their young.

In very wet ground, the stems stand a bit longer, fortified by the water that fills their stout, hollow stems. Sadly, even when nurtured with a steady supply of water, these gorgeous giants often experi ence a midsummer meltdown in windy gardens. It seems tempting to cut them to the ground and start over, but because they are mono- carpic, that usually won't work. Monocarps are plants that die after setting seed. Some are annuals; others can take years to mature and flower. Many, like angelica, are biennial, which means you get a year of great foliage, then a year of great bloom, then a fizzle-out to nothing. If you want to extend their garden life, you can cut back the top growth, preventing seed set. Sometimes this will fool a bien- nial into taking another year to flower.

Angelicas, though, are as peculiar as they are lovely, and one oddity involves rules about behavior. Most angelicas are biennials, but some are not. The same seed batch can produce both biennials and short-lived peren- nials, plants that persist for three or four years before vanishing. Sometimes this just seems to be so; an endless succession of seedlings give the impression of longevity, but what is really happening is that each year, at least one seedling comes to prominence. Some strains, in some gardens, are really more or less peren- nial, so if these plants behave inconsistently for you, don't feel you are doing something wrong when few if any plants survive over the long term.

Angelica archangelica

Angelica gigas

Angelica atropurpurea

For one thing, since angelica seeds itself with abandon, finding replacement babies is not exactly difficult. To get staggered crops of newcomers, buy plants two years in a row and let both go to seed.

That way, you will always have a few blooming sized plants on hand. I just let them seed about in the borders, moving or removing any I don't want. Because even young plants are huge, this carefree dispersal method isn't practical everywhere. Those with smaller gardens may prefer to sow some fresh seed in pots each year. Whether in pots or in the ground, young angelicas are highly attractive to slugs, which will swarm by the dozens over a full-grown plant. Careful baiting will protect enough seedlings to ensure a steady progression of plants, but it is remarkable how a huge crop can be reduced to a pathetic, tattered few without protection.

Hardy to Greenland, its northernmost habitat, this European herb also grows into central Asia, where it is joined by a dusky-flowered cousin, *Angelica gigas*. A splendidly showy creature, *A. gigas* made the horticultural hit parade a few years ago, when it was introduced to cultivation by modern-day plant hunter Barry Yinger. He found it growing in mountain meadows in Korea, where it flowers in a range of burgundy to ruddy black. Here, the best garden forms have dark stems and richly colored flowers, with enormous, sea green leaves veined in hot pink. This one is a bi- or triennial, taking two or three years to bloom and fade. A bit more compact than the archangel, this one generally tops out at about five feet, with dinner-plate-sized flower heads and salad-plate side-shoot blossoms. These, too, will be packed with seeds, which must be gathered fresh (while still green) and sown into pots, or the slugs will have them all. It seems amazing that such a lusty plant could be totally devoured by slugs, but so it is, and if your plants aren't replacing themselves, slugs are undoubtedly the culprit. Unless, of course, you are tidying away the stalks before the seed has ripened. Tidy is good, especially with such a potentially damaging plant, yet unless a few seed heads are left to mature, you'll forever be shelling out for seedlings at five bucks a pop.

Recently, the must-have plant has been the North American native called *Angelica atropurpurea*, or black Alexanders. It grows wild from Newfoundland down to Delaware, traveling west as far as Minnesota. Favoring swampy ground, it is a water hog in the garden, where it performs best in a soggy, boggy spot. Wild forms have midnight purple stems and dark green foliage veined and suffused with inky burgundy. Good selected garden forms have near-black foliage and warm purple stems, above which the umbels of white flowers gleam like little galaxies. Unlike its monocarpic cousin, black Alexanders is a true perennial. It rarely exceeds six feet in height, and its platter-sized umbels remind me of a muscular version of Queen Anne's lace. Long grown as a medicinal herb (favored for liver and spleen ailments), black Alexanders has never before attained high ornamental status. Neither has another dark angel, *A. atrisina*, whose finely cut foliage is even blacker than black Alexanders. The new appreciation for bold, strongly colored foliage plants promises to elevate this humble cooking herb and its kin to unimagined horticultural heights. Expect any and all of these murky forms to be rare and expensive for a year or two, but unless you are a gotta-have-it gardener, why not wait? Wisdom and an intimate understanding of the prolific nature of these plants suggests that in just a few seasons, they will be everywhere and quite reasonably priced.

Taking a Floral Flyer

 June

If May is full of promise, June really delivers, even after the peculiar kind of springs we have been experiencing lately. Whatever happened to normal springs, the kind that unfold in more or less linear fashion, progressing in a leisurely way from winter cold and damp to summer heat and dryer days? I distinctly recall lots of springs like that, yet my garden journals are full of plaintive commentaries about "this unusual year" and "this abnormal weather." Maybe the truth is that there is no such thing as a normal spring. Maybe a normal spring is fickle, fitful, and unpredictable. Maybe only in the imagination does spring come with grace and dignity, advancing smoothly without accompanying retreats.

Perhaps instead of saying, "This year, everything is behaving quite oddly," I should simply say, "This year, as usual, all is topsy-turvy in the borders," for so it generally is. One such spring, some plants were blooming early, while others dragged along, far behind their accustomed schedule. This was annoying, but all was not lost. The weather was weird and wacky, but nonetheless, ruffled peonies were chased by fragrant roses, and spiky delphiniums rose above fluffy lady's mantle. The evenings drew out, and the night air was rich

132

with the heady scent of honey locust. The garden gaps closed, and our foliage plants looked fresh and lustrous.

Despite this general festivity, one area of my garden was sulking and full of gaping holes. This part held heat lovers and borderline tender plants, many of them really successful only in a very mild year. Big clumps of copper red New Zealand flax (*Phormium* species) can make an exciting accent, their large, swordlike blades fanning out boldly among clouds of catmint (*Nepeta* species) and oriental poppies. The flexible, dipping wands of angels' fishing rod, *Dierama pulcherrimum*, may brighten the summer garden with clusters of rose and lilac bells dangling at the tips of five-foot stalks. Stunning South African honey bush, *Melianthus major*, is capable of producing huge, steel blue leaves with deeply serrated edges that can look smashing against a column of copper fennel or a midnight blue monkshood like *Aconitum bicolor* 'Spark's Variety'.

However, a sharp November frost, coupled with a soggy January, had left my borderline crowd looking less than impressive. The red flax looked insecure, its tattered leaves limp and battered. The angels' fishing rods were reduced from lusty clumps to a few pathetic shoots that did not seem likely to flower at all. The honey bush finally woke up and sent out new leaves, and by summer's end looked like an actual plant. In between these big guys were lots of smaller gaps filled only by tags, little white memorials to the departed. A couple of midnight red dahlias I thought

Aftermath of a hard winter in the garden

might have been able to winter over in the ground. Oh well. Some chocolate cosmos, murky burgundy in flower and smelling like Swiss Miss. Bye, dear. A really stunning gladiola called 'Zuni Chief', with enormous burnt orange and copper flowers. So long, chief.

In a sunnier garden with lighter, faster-draining soil, all of these plants would probably have come through the previous winter with little or no trauma. Indeed, when I really am determined to grow such plants on a more permanent basis, I amend their planting holes with quantities of extra grit or coarse sand to improve drainage.

A big handful of hydrated water-holding gel like Broadleaf P4 will not only act as a reservoir for thirsty roots all summer but also provide a measure of frost protection by holding the roots at 32 degrees. (Frozen hydrogel can't get colder than that.)

So why didn't these plants get the deluxe treatment? Partly, to learn how hardy a half-hardy plant really is. I often grow several each of such plants, treating one with extra care and siting the others in different situations to see how they fare. Also, it's valuable to learn how plants react to less-than-ideal settings as well as perfect ones. Much as I love gardening, it can't always come first on my daily to-do list. Until my young family matures a bit, I will still need to incorporate a high percentage of plants that can be relied upon to perform well with relatively little intervention.

Such research is not always focused on failure. No matter how rotten the weather, there are always some joyful because unexpected successes. A white jasmine (*Jasminum officinale*) that had filled the kitchen with questing shoots had been planted—more desperately than hopefully—at the foot of a purple-leaved hazel shrub. My garden is not really sunny enough for white jasmine, and I have lost several plants over the years. However, despite the damp winter and a dearth of sunshine, the jasmine was thick with buds.

Near it, a splendid clump of *Acidanthera murielae* rose in a lovely green sheaf of leaves, the flower buds already forming. This South African bulb is a late summer bloomer that is often carried away in a wet winter. This batch had been set in sand, and apparently the improved drainage was enough to coax those hydrophobic corms to stick around. Their emergence was a triumph indeed in this damp, clay-based garden. When the flowers open, they look like exotic white birds, perhaps herons, with elegantly flapping feathers (indeed, the bulbs used to be called peacock gladiolas and were sold as *Gladiolus bicolor*). Their scent is a haunting, spicy one that belongs to high summer, but late flowers can continue to appear into autumn, when the scent intensifies and deepens beautifully.

Even when such counterbalancing successes are few, there is always an upside to garden sorrow. Since my planting style is rather baroque, the beds can get quite crowded by midsummer. Plants that never had room to really spread their wings before flourish with less competition. Charming details long lost to view come back into the spotlight, better than ever. The garden as a whole settles into long-planned lines, and maturing backbone shrubs start to fill out their intended positions with élan. One lesson hard winters can teach us is that less quite often is more. The uncluttered garden has a stronger visual appeal than the collector's jumble so dear to my heart. The balance between clean design and floral abundance can be tricky to find and trickier yet to maintain. When design triumphs, too often it is at the cost of warmth and immediacy. When plant passion takes over, the garden has a distinct tendency toward chaos. Finding a rich and satisfying medium is my constant goal, yet the pendulum swings each year, each season, now weighted this way, now compensatorily shoved that way. This is the reality of dynamic balance; it is a flow, a flux, a constant, living cycle of change. Static patterns, however pleasing, don't make a garden thrum with life.

Some gardeners feel that the most telling tale of winter's aftermath is told by tags. Over time, every garden accumulates its share of plant tags that no longer accompany plants. This isn't failure, it's an opportunity to plant something there wasn't room for last year. The best thing to do after suffering a loss is to take a floral flyer; try something new, just for fun. If it works, great. If not, so what? If we never fail, we aren't really trying, for constant and consistent success means taking no risks. After all, we learn a lot from our failures. Garden risks are usually little ones, and nothing else so quickly expands the limits of what we know and can grow.

JULY

Wading in the Border

 July

While I was in the process of moving a garden, I received several interesting suggestions for moving plants in warm weather. I learned about one Samaritan who recently helped a friend move a garden from a rental property. Two hours after they finished, a team of hired weed whackers roared through the old garden. Unannounced by the landlord and unexpected by the gardeners, the whackers leveled everything in their wake. Fortunately, most of the border beauties had been salvaged first. Sadly, such experiences—or less lucky ones—are not uncommon. This is not because such landlords are spiteful, but because they simply don't get it. An amazing number of people do not relate to the concept of a garden as an entity.

A garden is much more than mere plants. It is more than the relationships among our plants, more than the manner, whether formal or casual, in which they are grouped. For passionate gardeners, gardens are in truth extensions of the self, living expressions of all we believe in and practice in daily life. Our gardens clearly encompass the physical facet of our relationship with plants, but they may extend well beyond that level. For most of us, the garden is a never-failing resource, a place where we find renewal and refreshment of spirit. Working quietly amongst our plants, grooming and planting, we find both comfort and energy. Acquiring plants is great fun, yet that absolutely ordinary contact with the earth brings deeper satisfactions than the most gluttonous buying spree. In truth, a living garden is far less about having than about doing and being.

I have always admired the spirit of renters who make beautiful gardens, not minding that they are just temporary. These brave hearts live with a truth the rest of us generally choose to ignore: All gardens are ephemera, lasting only as long as they have the active attention of their maker. This does not seem at all sad to me, but rather wonderful. It values beauty, process, and experience directly. The doing and being are acknowledged firmly to be as important as the end product. Any bone-deep gardener already knows all this. Why else do we spend more time hind end up in the border than hind end down on those artistic benches we strew around the garden for other people to sit on?

After my correspondent's close call, she went right to work with transplanting. Despite the midsummer heat, the plants moved well because this gal was well prepared. Here's her recipe for transplanting success: She fills buckets with "soup," a thin slurry made from manure, topsoil and water. This is especially smart when the ground is so dry. The slurry saturates quickly and clings to roots well. Opaque, it protects them from sun better than plain water, thus reducing transplant shock.

On hot days, even a few minutes of direct sun can fry delicate roots. It's vital to protect plants during every step of a move. Indeed, if you don't need to move plants, this is not the time to do it. If, however, it's a question of do or die, you might as well give it a try. The following precautions can make the difference between surprising success and frying failure.

The minute you dig those poor endangered plants up, plunge them directly into buckets of manure soup (or water). If there is any shade on your work site, keep the buckets of slurry in the shade and move all new transplants there as soon as you can. (Immediately is good.) If you have a lot of moving, to do, things will progress better if you can round up some helpful friends. In a hot, dry site, setting up a tarp from the back of the car could provide some temporary shade if necessary.

If facilities are available, you or a buddy can tuck your new transplants straight into containers. If you can't do this on site, do it as soon as you get home. Either way, water them well, submerging the pots into buckets to be sure the soil is truly saturated. In summer, potting soil is apt to be very dry and often quite hot to boot. Traumatized roots are very vulnerable, and hot potting soil could finish off what our hasty shovels began. To avoid toxic shock, keep your potting soil in the shade (if you can). If you can't, plunging your plants will wet them thoroughly and the subsequent evaporation will cool them off nicely. Keep the new transplants in shade for a minimum of several weeks, creating it with cheesecloth, old screens, or a beach umbrella if necessary.

Transplanting

Even with the best treatment, plants moved during active growth often flag or collapse. If they do, trim off all flower buds and any sagging new growth. Keep their soil moist but not sodden, and protect them from sun and wind. When they perk up (usually in a day or two), you can gradually allow them more sun. It may be three weeks or more before some transplants can take full sun. Continue to treat the slow to recover as convalescents, coddling them until they start to produce new growth.

My enterprising correspondent reports that she and her friend stored their booty in a kiddie wading pool with holes poked in the bottom, and suggested that since I too was trying to move a garden in the heat, I might do the same. Now, I actually own any number of old wading pools with holes in the bottom (this is not an item that's easy to get rid of). While I had not considered planting them, the idea has merit; it's practical, cheap, and dead easy, given a large supply of decent soil or compost.

The idea offers fascinating design challenges as well. What colorist effects are suggested by aqua whales and bubble-gum-pink hippos? One ex-pool is shaped like a gigantic frog, goggle eyes and all. Here, the theme would be the thing; water lilies leap to mind (got to plug those holes), with an edging of frog spawn plant, *Euphorbia palustris*. This lovely chartreuse spurge is a riverside dweller, so that works.

If such concepts seem too frivolous (or tacky—go ahead and say it), there is a simple but elegant solution. Just trim your pool with low bamboo screening and it will look classy enough for a Smith & Hawken catalog (or at the very least, a luau). Whatever their artistic qualities, wading pools really can be terrific stopgap planters. Necessity is indeed the mother of invention, and when extreme conditions prevail, such ingenuity becomes invaluable.

If the solution needs to be a bit more lasting—weeks instead of days—a bit more preparation is required. Wading pools will work best for longer-term plant storage if you cover their bottoms with several inches of gravel before adding soil. (Where weight is an issue, substitute plastic/foam packing peanuts.) This promotes better drainage and air flow to plant roots. Toss in some worms as well, for even splendid soil compacts quickly without tunneling worms to keep it open.

Bio-cool Gardening
Boosts Productivity

 July

Last time the guru of bio-intensive gardening was in town, I got an earful of hot tips to pass along. John Jeavons's name is most familiar to organic gardeners, who probably own a copy of his masterwork, *How to Grow More Vegetables* (Ten Speed Press, revised 1995, $16.95). This pithy and practical manual has steered some 300,000 people through the intricacies of a way of gardening that often becomes a way of life.

"Bio-intensive gardening makes more sense every day," says Jeavons. "It's fun, it's easy, it's healthy, it's beautiful, and it's effective. It saves the gardener's time and energy as well as resources like water, seeds, and fertilizers."

Born in Northern California, bio-intensive is a fusion between eastern and western gardening schools. From the French Intensive and the English Biodynamic schools comes the emphasis on deep soil preparation and mulches that nourish the soil. Ancient Chinese agricultural practices contribute the concepts of bio-sustainability: Everything that comes out of the garden goes back in, one way or another. Everything the garden needs can be supplied from its own abundance.

Twenty-five years ago, an English transplant to the Bay Area named Alan Chadwick brought this young school into being. A dedicated gardener, he learned all he could about soil and plant growth, studied various systems of agriculture, and explored gardening techniques worldwide. Back in the garden, he put two and two together and started getting eight or ten. Some people call it synergy; he called it bio-intensive, feeling that the combined system capitalized on natural life processes. Other people tried his methods with similarly effective results. Before long, a bio-intensive movement was launched that has traveled all over the world.

John Jeavons has studied and practiced bio-intensive gardening for years, adding to the pool of information that guides newcomer and novice toward mastery. He teaches classes in his own community and all over the country, and his book is considered the basic training manual for this extraordinarily productive way of gardening. Within weeks of getting started, proponents can be growing beautiful and nourishing food. You don't need acreage to try out these theories, either. Many bio-intensive fans are feeding their families out of small plots in ordinary urban backyards.

"These bio-intensive techniques are especially welcome in the Third World, where resources are often limited," notes Jeavons. You don't need to be a botanist or have horticultural training in order to apply bio-intensive methods in your home garden. Though the charts and tables included in the book delight techies who love precise directions and interlacing rules, the seemingly indigestible mass of information can daunt a beginner. If Jeavons's book looks confusing to you, take a deep breath and just plunge in. The water's fine, and all the basic principles are very simple. "The bio-intensive method is really based on five steps," he explains. Although his book deals with them in depth, they can be summed up briefly.

1. Prepare garden soil deeply.

The first step is to double-dig the beds. This means loosening the soil to a depth of at least two feet, or two shovel depths. The point is to incorporate more air into the soil, which Jeavons calls "one of most important missing ingredients in agriculture." This is hard work, but it only needs to be done once. Thereafter, feeding mulches keep the soil in excellent condition.

2. Use compost.

A chunk of compost the size of a quarter contains six billion microbes that feed our plants by feeding the soil. When we recycle the garden into compost, nutrients that would be lost are returned. The more varied the raw plant material, the richer the microbial mix in the finished compost. Since more than six thousand different microbial life forms exist, each favoring certain plants, we can encourage microbial diversity by growing the greatest possible variety of crops. When we mulch with complex, plant-based composts, we nurture our soil, which in turn feeds our plants better than chemical fertilizers can.

Bio-intensive gardening

3. Space plants closely.

Bio-intensive practices call for tight spacing, so that plants just barely overlap on another at maturity. The result is a living mulch that keeps the ground moist and cool. Not only does this conserve water, but it turns the top two inches of soil into an ideal miniclimate for healthy microbial life. Best of all, it forms a humidity bubble that captures carbon dioxide, which plants breathe in and convert to oxygen. For plants, having lots of available CO_2 is like breathing pure oxygen for humans; it invigorates them and makes them grow more strongly.

4. Use companion planting.

The idea that certain plants like or hate others seems silly, yet it is founded in fact. "We can't always isolate the chemical factors at work," Jeavons explains, "but we can measure the effects of companion planting." A classic is Bibb lettuce planted in a 4:1 ratio with spinach. Tuck one spinach plant next to every fourth Bibb lettuce seedling, and not only will all the plants involved grow larger than those grown alone, but the companions will taste appreciably better. Green beans and strawberries are similarly synergistic, but don't plant peas or beans near onions, or both crops will be reduced in quality and weight.

5. Use the whole system.

It isn't enough to try a couple of the ideas, Jeavons cautions. "This is a whole system, and though all of its parts are useful alone, none are as effective that way. It isn't about cramming lots of plants in the ground, but about creating a self-sustaining system. All the hard work comes in the beginning, but once it's set up properly, it's child's play to keep it going."

Bio-intensive is worth a try not only for the yields, which are often four to six times larger than usual. "The system requires much less energy to perpetuate, and uses far fewer resources," Jeavons asserts. "Water, for instance: If all farming and gardening in California were done bio-intensively, there would be no drought. One year's worth of water would last for seven or eight years, and the yields would be greater as well."

If you need more convincing, Jeavons suggests you try a tiny test plot and see for yourself how well it works. "Even a three- by three-foot plot will amaze you with its productivity. After one season, most people become total enthusiasts. This is exciting to watch, and just plain terrific fun to do." Having experimented with both French intensive and bio-intensive methods in the past, I can assure you that everything he asserts is quite true. If you want to take a bio-intensive flyer without making a huge commitment, make your bed in a large tub or container (this eliminates the double digging) and load it with good soil and compost. Follow the tips and techniques in Jeavons's book, and your patio pocket hanky garden will be producing salads and side dishes all summer.

Successful First Gardens

 July

Not long ago, friends faced with an empty yard and no gardening experience called for help. They wanted a garden that would be interesting all year round, yet would require very little maintenance and no horticultural skill to keep it healthy. This is the kind of challenge designers adore, because working with a perfectly blank slate allows terrific freedom of choice in terms of plants. Also, people with no expectations are overjoyed with whatever success they experience—anything that lives for them is a little miracle. By simply filling their yard with an assortment of solid performers, the designer can create a source of a great deal of pleasure. The lucky ones may even spark an interest in the owners that eventually becomes a lifelong passion, for thus may true gardeners be born.

My friends' front yard was a thirty- by twenty-foot rectangle, divided down one side by a cracked, narrow concrete walkway. This they broke up with sledgehammers (it's hard work, but great therapy) and removed to the backyard, where we recycled it into low retaining walls for a vegetable bed. Concrete chunks can be set with the flat sides out, making a smooth edge, and their texture is surprisingly attractive. Set a few tumbling herbs, like creeping mints and prostrate rosemary, to clamber over them, and such walls can look mellowed and comfortable in very short order.

In the front garden, my friends replaced the old concrete with a more generous path. We decided to make it the width of the porch steps, which were six feet across, for a cleaner, more open look. The path was set with handsome bluestone slabs, framed in by treated wooden beams. This immediately created an inviting entryway that made the lot look less narrow and squidgy despite the increased width. Because the proportions were better, the path looked more in scale with the house.

Before you design a new garden, it's good to assess what might already be available in the way of plants or structure. In this case, the only plant was a badly pruned but not unattractive dogwood (*Cornus florida*), which stood to the left of the front porch, centered in the narrower, shadier side of the yard. It needed to be limbed up and thinned a bit but was otherwise in good shape. There was nothing else alive at all but ratty lawn, which was struggling, having been inadvertently poisoned by the guy of the house (surprise!), who was trying to get rid of the weeds. In his zeal, he overdid the herbicide, but that lawn was no loss. It would, however, have been very easy to remove it by hand, without any poison. Here we tilled up the sorry remains, adding in a ten-yard load of aged manure and twenty bags of mushroom compost.

We then raked out all the chunks of grass roots (which float to the surface when you rake) and removed all the weeds as well. To avoid more weeds coming in, we mulched the whole yard to a depth of about four inches. The owners bought finely shredded bark, which is inexpensive and attractive but does rob the soil of nitrogen as it breaks down. Because we had already amended with manure and compost, I wasn't too worried about the nitrogen loss. We did, however, add a handful of alfalfa pellets to each planting as we worked. This gives an extra burst of nitrogen, especially when combined with manure. Also, we all used thin rubber gloves (the inexpensive kind sold for dishwashing) when mulching, because bark products are usually chock-full of splinters.

Last of all, the wider, sunnier side of the yard was bisected with a wide path of flat but irregularly shaped stones. I personally dislike walking on or looking at crazy paving of this type, but the owners both wanted it and planned to grow a variety of creeping thymes over and among the pavers. We laid out the new path in an arc that led to a small dirt path that ran behind the house and gave access to the backyard. The mouth of this side path was framed with a timbered arbor, over which we hung an evergreen Chinese clematis for year-round cover and winter fragrance. The crazy paving path created two large, gently curving beds in the sunny part of the lawn, which were mulched and left ready to be planted. The shaded, dogwood side already had a little path, so it was treated as a single ten-by twenty-foot bed, which we prepped in the same manner.

Next, my fearless friends constructed a six-foot-high wooden fence to create more privacy and give the garden definite boundaries. (This project was less fun than whacking concrete but equally good as action therapy and a character builder for gardener and garden alike.) When all was ready, we took a day to place about a hundred key plants, which the two of them planted over the next few weeks. They were amazed to see a bunch of plants in pots become transformed into an instant garden, simply by being placed in lovely combinations and communities. I gave

Recipe for a first garden

them a watering schedule and showed them how to plant so that the old soil level was matched in the ground. They also promised to mulch each plant and give it the alfalfa pellets as planned.

A year later, the garden was healthy and thriving, and both of the owners had become active gardeners. A few plants had died, but they were adding bulbs and perennials—plants of their own choosing—to fill the gaps, and the garden was becoming more their own with each addition.

Aside from the ideal weather, the reason this little garden succeeded so well is that all the plants were chosen to perform well in that site with little encouragement. Since my friends' situation—part shade, mostly full sun, with lean subsoil that barely supported grass—was quite typical of urban lots, the same recipe has proven useful for other beginning garden makers as well. Here, in brief, is a Recipe for a First Garden:

1. One quarter of the plants should be evergreens, some broadleaved, some needled conifers. In a big garden, these will be small trees and big shrubs; in a tiny space, use one or two dwarf trees and medium to compact shrubs. These are placed around the perimeter to frame and define the garden all year round. We used fastigiate Irish junipers and strawberry tree (*Arbutus unedo*) for the framework.

2. Half of the remaining evergreen plants are compact or dwarf forms that are clustered in the borders for year-round interest. Choose these for great natural shapes and textural appeal. These are grouped into compatible islands of evergreens, which can be surrounded by bulbs and perennials.

3. In design terms, all gardens need a centerpiece; here, the shaggy old dogwood was opened up by removing all ground-sweeping branches to reveal its graceful trunk. Where there is no ready-made centerpiece, a similarly sculptural small tree such as the weeping white crabapple (*Malus* 'Green Jade') would do nicely.

4. The rest of the plants are easygoing yet noninvasive perennials, with preference given to those with extended bloom period, good foliage, interesting seed heads, and graceful maturity. Though it's fun to create knockout high-summer combinations, include as many off-season bloomers as possible so that the flow of living color continues through the seasons. Also be sure to include plenty of grasses, big and small, which provide exceptional variety of color and texture over time.

5. After the initial planting and settling down period, any gaps are filled in with bulbs and more perennials, with emphasis on off-season color (early and late bloomers).

Basic as this sounds, the results can be truly spectacular. Because the emphasis is on form, texture, and foliage color, the plants weave themselves into wondrous tapestries with very little help from us. The trick is to group plants companionably, so that they can merge when in full growth, yet allow them enough elbow room to develop their natural shapes. Fortunately, if a few months down the road it becomes obvious that the plants are spaced awkwardly, all you have to do is move them. This is less easy with larger plants, especially when established, so move these as soon as you see a spatial problem developing.

Hundreds of plants could fill the required role, and finding them is great fun. To get started, consult local nurseryfolk, and spend some time cruising nurseries and gardens, making notes about plants that please your eye. If you need help, hire a garden designer to work up a list that would be appropriate for your site. In the meantime, go ahead and start taking up that ratty lawn (if you don't have one, maybe your neighbor does). Till and amend and mulch away, thinking all the while about what you would like to be looking at where the lawn once was. That way, when you are ready to begin to explore the art of gardening, your canvas will be stretched and primed. It may seem odd to begin a garden with soil prep rather than by choosing plants, but dirt work pays off many times over. Remember, as you work along, that great gardens begin with great soil.

Sociable New Climbers

 July

I love vines. I mean, I *really* love vines. To a fault. For
years, I bought every creeper, crawler, scrambler, and rambler I saw that seemed to want to come home with me. Over
time, that added up to a lot of plants. After nine years of cultivation, my old garden was so utterly jammed with climbers
that there was no room to hang a newcomer. Every suitable
upright plant (and a few that were truthfully not very suitable) was decked and draped and festooned with a vine or
scrambler or rambler of some description.

In the early years, the effect was quite pretty. From early
summer until fall, every tree and shrub in the garden was
abloom with borrowed blossom. Sometimes the flowers of
the trees and shrubs were joined by friendly neighbors who
wove webs of leaf and flower through them, and sometimes
plain Jane plants were given moments of glory by visiting
vines. As time wore on, however, the garden started to look
less and less charming and more and more like the ruins of
Miss Havisham's wedding. Instead of Dickensian cobwebs,
my woody plants were buried under a rampant mass of
greenery.

In some cases, such veiling was a blessing, because many
of the elderly framework trees were far past their prime.

Trees that block an ugly view, screen the house from the road, or disguise the neighbor's satellite dish may not be dispensable even if they are far from shapely. In such instances, evergreen climbers in particular can be an extremely useful addition to the picture. In my garden, a goodly number of vines were doing double duty, providing their own beauty while masking the lack of somebody else's. Just as often, though, the clambering guests simply obliterated the natural shape of the poor hosts.

Since then, I've learned some restraint. Indeed, leaving the garden and all my plants behind broke a long chain of acquisition for me. As I started over, this new attitude was reflected in the plantings. In my new garden, no tree or shrub is asked to carry more than one passenger to the skies. Indeed, several have no sociable climbers at all, and look the better for this solitude. Okay, there are still a lot of climbers, but they represent the cream of the crop, not whatever happened to catch my eye.

This time, instead of buying every untried clematis I find, I have kept myself to a chosen few. The trellised deck holds a vigorous Chinese *Clematis armandii*, which bloomed like a fragrant, creamy cloud in February and March. Given a huge hole full of good dirt, in a position where its roots are in shade but its leaves and flowers are in the sun, this great scrambler is easy to please. We trim off any deadwood each year, lest it turn into a snarled tangle, but otherwise, there is very little to do but give it plenty of water while in active growth. A handful of manure and alfalfa pellets give it a boost in spring, and I repeat the dose in early fall, when important root growth is taking place underground.

Now it is trying happily to cover the overhead arbor, which it will

Chinese Clematis armandii

Golden hop vine

Chinese Clematis serratifolia

Clematis alpina

Lady Hillingdon rose

Lady Banks rose

Morning glory

Balloon vine

Climbing maurandyas (Asarina)

Sweet potatoes

Creeping gloxinia

share with a golden hop vine. This last has large, palmate leaves that are clear gold in spring and fade to softer chartreuse in summer. Tiny flowers are concealed by showy, dangling bracts that are reputed to promise sweet dreams when stuffed into pillows. In the ground, golden hop is a serious thug, able to enrobe a large tree in just a few seasons. In my old garden, it ate first a laburnum, then a blue spruce. A year later, it discovered the telephone pole. Hop vines take to telephones like a teenager. In no time, it was off and running, and I would get calls from plaintive neighbors saying, "I have a pretty yellow vine over here and was wondering, is it yours?" The lesson is to plant it where it has room to roam. If you can't give it that much scope, you must confine its roots. Grown in pots or tubs (bigger is better), hops become much more mannerly without losing the natural exuberance that make them joyful creatures to be around.

Below the vine-clad deck, a large katsura, imported with great effort from a friend's garden, holds the delicate, lacy-leaved *Clematis serratifolia*, whose lemony bells smell appropriately of citrus. It blooms in bursts from high summer into autumn, when its netted stems may be covered with thousands of nodding golden bells. After the flowers fade, they are followed by silky tufts of floss that turn clematis seed heads into charming ornaments. This is another charming Chinese clematis, but this one is deciduous. Its long arms can be allowed to wander at will through a hedge or into a large shrub.

Across the wide gravel path, a good sized spindletree, *Euonymus europaea*, is swagged with spring-blooming *Clematis alpina*, a pale form called 'White Moth' that glimmers like its namesake in the early twilight of March. It also holds a summer bloomer, the sugar pink 'Little Nell', but that's not my fault; the tree came to me that way. The plants have grown together so that it would be quite hard to remove anybody from this ménage à trois, and I'm not even going to try.

Around the corner by the front porch, a climbing Lady Hillingdon rose is trying valiantly to cover one of the deck posts, but this garden (perhaps this climate?) is not quite warm enough for her ladyship. Her amber and butterscotch blossoms are so lovely I can't resist trying to grow her, but will probably end up removing her to a sunnier setting. Meanwhile, I have better hopes for the Lady Banks rose on the other side of the deck. *Rosa banksiae* makes good company, because the long (to thirty-foot) stems are nearly thornless. In spring, it carries a flock of small, single white flowers that have the same heady scent as Parma violets. This one also likes a sheltered, sunny position, where its buds won't be blasted by late frosts.

Though my new garden is small, there is room for a lot more climbers. (At least, to my eye there is.) However, rather than filling all available space quickly with large woody vines, I decided to try out some of the new annual climbers appearing in local nurseries. One of my favorites is a dusky morning glory called 'Niala's Black'. I have grown this many times and am struck each season by its mysterious coloration. It is threaded through a young golden hypericum, where it holds up a succession of purple-throated, midnight colored trumpets for the delectation of the hummingbirds.

The cutting bed is full of hopeful young shrubs, all of which can easily bear an annual vine. A young scouler willow holds the variegated morning glory called *Ipomoea* × *imperialis* 'Tie-Dye', which produced lots of big foliage with swirling, creamy patterns, but no flowers. (I saw these elsewhere, though; they were huge, soft blue, and swirled with cream.) Its sibling, *I.* × *i.* 'Chocolate', began blooming at the end of June, showing off big blossoms of cafe-au-lait that look terrific against the reddish-purple foliage of a youthful purple hazel.

New to me is the balloon vine, *Cardiospermum halicacabum*. Its long tendrils of cutleaf foliage are decked with miniature white flowers, after which appear the balloons, inflated seedpods that hold glossy black seeds neatly marked with white hearts. In its tropical American home, it can reach thirty feet in a season. Here it will do no such thing, and I merely hope to see those pretty seedpods before frost cuts down its delicate, tangled stems.

Some years ago, I grew climbing maurandyas with velvety purple snapdragon-flowers. Now they are called *Asarina*, and quite a few good forms are available. I'm trying *Asarina scandens* 'Midnight Blue', a murky color that looks great with flat, hot reds and oranges or bronze and copper foliage. Softer forms called 'Sky Blue' and

'Rose' would make great basket-drippers or modest scramblers for a fine-textured trellis, and can also be fun used to decorate the holding beds with a froth of lacework.

I used to grow a stunning sweet potato called *Ipomoea batatas* 'Blackie' as a houseplant, bringing it out for the summer to enjoy such sun as my shady garden offered. This new garden is far lighter, and I have been trying a number of sweet potatoes that are being sold as annual vines. All can be kept alive indoors if not allowed to get too cold, for their tubers will rot at the merest touch of frost. The glorious 'Blackie', whose stubby-fingered leaves are really the color of the night, cascades over my rock wall, in company with the thundercloud purple buds of *Sedum* 'Vera Jameson'. This wall gets quite warm, which suits the slow-growing sweet potatoes nicely; in less favored spots, they simply refuse to grow at all. Here, tangles of bright yellow 'Margarita' mingle with a golden mat of creeping *Veronica austriaca* ssp. *teucrium* 'Trehane', whose brilliant blue flowers contrast vividly with the lemon-lime sweet potato foliage.

A few years ago I was thrilled to find a single plant of pink and cream variegated 'Tricolor'. Now, Blackie's cousins are everywhere. I bought half a dozen of the pink and cream variegated 'Tricolor' and crammed them in a hanging basket, where they get lots of direct light and extra reflected heat from the white house walls. They thrive here, while the ones on the wall merely extend a cautious stem or two. The last kind I am growing is called 'Variegata' and is said to have green and white foliage. Mine is a drab shade of green with some dim splotches of gray. Perhaps it needs better conditions to strut its stuff. I had hoped it would provide a crisp foil for Blackie's subfusc foliage. Maybe I should try growing it as I recently saw it, in a warm garden where the black stems poured down a cobalt blue wall in a stunning display.

Another plant I am more accustomed to thinking of as a house denizen is also making the rounds as a summer annual. Creeping gloxinia (*Asarina erubescens*) has sticky, hairy foliage with fat, rosy flowers that are considerably larger than the others. This makes a delightful pot plant and can be wintered over in a cool greenhouse or on a sunny windowsill. I've never grown it as an outdoor vine before, but when I spotted it at the nursery, it seemed to call my name. Oh dear. Is this a good sign or a bad one?

In years when your early annuals are still underperforming in midsummer, disheartened by wind and weather, it's not too late to try a few more. In a wet, cool year, we can keep on planting as long as we like. If summer heat ever does arrive, healthy but late-planted annuals (or perennials, for that matter) are likely to outshine those planted at the "right" time.

Tropicalismo for
Temperate Gardens

 July

One of the hottest trends in haute garden making is a sizzling, color-drenched style called tropicalismo. This exuberant school celebrates dramatic plants, exotic foliage, and vivid contrasts of hue and form. Over the past decade, it has progressed steadily northward from south of the border, where gardening with tropicals often involves using native plants. Along the way, stopovers in both San Francisco and Seattle gave this salsa-based school a distinctly American twist.

These days, adventurous northwestern gardeners are playing around with all kinds of tropicals, not just South Americans. African banana trees mingle with spiky New Zealand flax, Chinese windmill palms, Tasmanian tree ferns, and European giant reed grasses. Like the Brazilian tropicalismo musical movement, which begat the fashion for world music, garden tropicalismo incorporates plants from everywhere, anywhere, so long as they enjoy one another's company and provide the visual effect the gardener is looking for. Like those complex baseline beats that make world music both catchy and memorable, tropicalismo relies on repetition of form with multiple variations. Most of these gardens are based more on plant form and foliage pattern than on flowers. Though flowers do play their part (and often a significant one), it is the flow and interplay of shape and texture that provide both constancy and greatest interest.

As a result, plants with fascinating foliage are definitely horticulturally hot. Even those huge, paddle-leaved cannas that were once an avant gardening no-no are hip again. That goes double for cannas with striped or ruddy foliage. Thanks to their association with the tight, meticulous, and usually fussy bedding out beloved of the Victorians, bold plants like cannas were widely stigmatized as "obvious," not to say outright tacky. Well, closet canna fans are in luck. Today, the bigger and bolder the better. All over the Northwest, modest plants in cool pastels are being ousted by big guys in blazing sun colors. Indeed, several famous English gardeners are also jumping on the tropical bandwagon (though not, of course, giving us any credit for the idea).

Those who could never quite grasp the carefully toned progressions of tint in those English-style gardens are greeting this new movement with happy relief. Contrasts that require analysis by spectrometer to detect are no longer de rigueur. The large scale and generous scope of tropicalismo make these gardens tremendous fun for anybody to create. Like any style, this one is subject to interpretation. Some folks weave hardy tropicals into lush green havens where foliage patterns create most of the visual excitement. Other people make brilliantly colorful, stimulating gardens full of color shocks and surprises.

Tropicalismo

Spiky devil's club

Wild sumacs

Rhododendrons

Japanese maples

False hellebores

Naturally, this look isn't for everybody, nor does it work effortlessly with every style of architecture. However, even a quiet woodland garden can gain significant visual impact from an infusion of plants with outsized foliage. They don't have to be tender (and expensive) tropicals to work. Indeed, good candidates include anything with exotic-looking leaves, from rhododendrons to rhubarbs. Good old *Fatsia japonica* is making a comeback, as are those once-reviled gold-spotted aucubas (another fine plant tainted by Victorian excess). Kitchen gardens contribute huge angelicas, lacy lovage, and feathery fennel. Pacific gunneras share border space readily with northwestern skunk cabbages. Fancy Chinese ribes meet their match in our maple-like native thimbleberry as well as in the raspberry-colored clusters of native currant (*Ribes sanguineum*) and the hot orange of salmonberry. These are brilliantly used in a garden on Vancouver Island, where the dangling salmon fruits bob in front of a mass of dark purple allium. The onion heads and the rounded fruits play off each other delightfully, both in color and form, making an unforgettable picture.

Not surprisingly, tropicalismo requires some adjustments from both garden and gardener. If your present garden is modeled after one of the English icon styles, whether cottage or estate garden, or if it incorporates elements from formal European styles, you will want to think your approach out carefully. In an artlessly gay cottage garden, a sudden influx of tree ferns will look both improbable and foolish. You could, however, work tree ferns—or red banana trees, or figs—into an Italianate garden quite easily. One main difference to work toward will be the overall balance between hardscape—the man-made elements such as patios, terraces, arbors, and pergolas—and plants. In the tropicalismo style, plants are ascendant, whereas English and European traditions require that the hand of man be the clear winner.

It has been argued that tropical plants look ill at ease against our native landscapes, but that point can be debated both ways. I would claim that urban gardens can be made in any style at all, since the visual context is nearly always man-made and rectilinear, with few or no natural cues or context to work with. In such settings, tropicalismo is a highly effective means for creating a convincing fantasy garden that instantly whisks us away from the city streets to paradise. In older neighborhoods and suburbs, there is often an established tree line to play off. The more this includes native trees, the more tropicalismo is likely to work. If that tree line includes garry oaks or madronas, we are definitely in luck, for both look as exotic as any plant coming from the Australian outback or out of Africa.

So, too, do our native ash (*Fraxinus latifolia*) and cascara (*Rhamnus purshianus*). Both are fine-textured trees that look like hot-country inhabitants.

Should we be gardening in or near native woodlands, we are doubly in luck. Not only can we use those red-barked madronas and twisting oaks as reference, but we can draw on the large pool of native shrubs and perennials that have large or striking foliage. Native elders (*Sambucus*) are long fingered and boldly shaped and provide pleasing contrast with heavier broadleaved evergreens like *Garrya elliptica*, whose dangling catkins provide additional winter interest. In sunny sites, native manzanitas and kinnikinnicks (*Arctostaphylos* species) play the role that glossy salal (*Gaultheria shallon*) and fernleaved Oregon grape (*Mahonia repens*) fill in woodland settings.

If you have a damp, shady spot, consider creating a bed around spiky devil's club (*Oplopanax horridus*), a native woodlander that looks as though it came from Mars. This punk plant has more spines than a porcupine and holds its large, maple-like leaves horizontally, the better to spike innocent passersby. Resolutely martial in character, it is nonetheless a stunner to showcase anywhere suitable that you want an emphatic plant. Don't, however, place it near a path where it may be accidentally touched. Unless you are trying to create a natural barrier hedge, this is definitely a plant for the background, to be admired from a respectful distance.

Less threatening (except in its toxic "poison" forms), wild sumacs have shaggy, fringed foliage that powerfully suggests the tropics. Many have furry stems and colorful winter bark as well as exciting fall color, providing a full year's interest for mixed borders. Although they look like escapees from Hawaii, our North American natives are rock hardy and highly adaptable in garden settings. Our Northwestern native sumac, *Rhus glabra*, is a glorious shrub that can exceed twelve feet when happy. It is, however, all too inclined to be happy, and unless your garden is very large, you will probably want to substitute a less rampant species. You can also grow this lovely thug in a large container, cutting it back hard each spring to encourage outsized foliage. Treated in this manner, it will remain humbler in height, but the leaves may achieve three or more feet in length. In small gardens, the fragrant lemon sumac, *Rhus aromatica*, is a better bet. Native to the eastern states and Canada, this low grower makes mats two or three feet tall, spreading as wide as you like, but more readily controlled than the far-ranging *R. glabra*. It too colors beautifully in autumn, and its cutleaf form, 'Laciniata', glows like gilded fringe in fall. The fragrant flowers appear in summer, the color of lemons and offering a strong and sweetly citrusy scent.

While our native rhododendrons are not especially exotic looking, they do mingle readily with bolder, more brazen cousins. The tremendous leaves of *R. macabeanum* and species like *R. bureavii* with rusty indumentum fit right in with our native evergreen huckleberries, *Vaccinium ovatum*, whose glossy new growth is the exact same shade of cinnamon red. Indeed, huckleberries and almost any rhododendron species look perfectly at home when planted together, as do many azaleas. I choose these last for flaming fall color, planting them where they are pretty in spring, unobtrusive in summer, and can blaze out from the borders come autumn.

Like our native bigleaf maple (*Acer circinatum*), Japanese maples can look extremely exotic and will quickly find a spot in a tropicalismo shade garden. Some of the tiny-leaved forms mimic our native deciduous red huckleberries (*Vaccinium parvifolium*) so precisely in form, habit, and texture that recognition of their true identity comes as a mild shock. Again like our own native species (all of which are garden worthy), Japanese maples of all descriptions look very comfortable when grown in native woodland settings, blending easily with their surroundings but bringing an infusion of additional color and a satisfying variety of foliage shapes.

If you want to jump right in and add some instant oomph to your garden, start browsing local nurseries for bold foliage plants. On a recent trip to Reflective Gardens Nursery in exotic Poulsbo, I found rare ligularias, *Rodgersia podophylla* 'Rotlaub', and extra-large-leaved rhododendrons, which work wonderfully in tropicalismo settings. This fine nursery also stocks a good selection of Northwest natives, many of which have noteworthy foliage despite not being of tropical origin. False hellebores (*Veratrum californicum*) can reach six or seven feet in time, their great stalks rising from mucky woodlands, trimmed with long, pleated leaves and spumes of creamy green flowers. Greener still are those of *V. viride*, a similarly robust character that also likes damp soils and dappled light.

Reflective Gardens also offers an enticing (and reasonably priced) collection of arisaemas and other aroids with marvelous, skinny-fingered foliage and strange, hooded flowers. Towering Himalayan lily

RESOURCES

REFLECTIVE GARDENS NURSERY
24329 NE SNOW HILL LANE
POULSBO, WA 98370
360/598-4649

relatives, the fabled cardiocrinums will soar ten feet and more, each stem decked with waxen white trumpets. They also provide an intriguing assortment of species peonies with splendidly exotic-looking foliage that colors hotly or turns softly golden in fall, as well as stunning seedpods that burst brightly, revealing glowing black seeds nestled in fuchsia pink silk.

Even if you don't elect to replace your roses with red bananas and palm trees, a few emphatic foliage plants will make your garden more dramatic, not to mention photogenic. With all the increasing national interest in Northwest gardens, yours, too, could grace the front of a glossy magazine. Next stop, Hollywood!

AUGUST

Troubled Plants:
How to Know When It's Over

 August

How can we know when it's time to stop nursing sulky plants and toss them out? How long should we be patient with their lack of progress or failure to thrive? At what point are we justified in boldly offing a faltering plant that might/could/should recover? These provocative questions have philosophical ramifications that extend well beyond the garden.

Let's look at one particular instance: the case of a gardener whose fairly new shrubs aren't doing well. "Fairly new" is a loose term that could cover anything from days to months or even a couple of years, depending on how you experience the flow of time. Gardeners tend to be long sighted and patient, which makes us underestimate at times. Let's assume these troubled shrubs have been in the garden for less than a year.

There are many reasons why new plants might be faring poorly. The first question to ask is whether these plants have received consistent, good care since their arrival. Indeed, a whole series of guilt-inducing questions can be posed: Were their beds well prepared before planting? Were the planting holes generously dug and well amended with manure and compost? Are the plants placed at the right depth, their

167

rootballs neither smothered deep below ground level nor left high and dry several inches above the soil line? Were they watered in well when planted, then kept scrupulously moist ever since?

If our conscience is clear, as it probably is, we can look farther afield for reasons. How did the plants look when we bought them? Perhaps their problems were not yet full blown but incipient. Persistent yellowing of leaves, browning or crisping of leaf margins, and a variety of disfigurements may be caused by disease. Many local nurseries can identify problems and suggest solutions if shown a few troubled leaves. If not, call your local extension agent or Master Gardener service.

The difficulty may have practical rather than pathological causes. Rootbound plants can have a hard time getting past their own tangles. Those tight rootballs need to be carefully teased apart before transplanting. When this is impossible, they should at least be scuffed a bit, which involves breaking some of those wiry outer roots. This horrifies the gentle in spirit, yet if nothing is done we may well hoick the dead plant out of the ground several painful years later only to find the original rootball intact. The poor plants can't always set themselves free, despite cushy new surroundings.

Brand new plants bought in summer heat may get a little ratty despite proper planting and care. Spring-bought plants that looked healthy initially could easily flag when a cold, late spring is followed by a suddenly hot summer. Give newcomers the benefit of the doubt, for weather stress can make anybody look lusterless. If the heat is on, as soon as it's over, try digging up those faltering plants to check their roots. If you see signs of healthy new root growth, replace them tenderly and leave them alone. Next spring, you'll probably be rewarded with refurbished plants.

New plants, shaky or not, should always be well readied for winter. Give particular attention to young broadleaved evergreens, which are especially susceptible to disfiguring wind or frost burn if stressed. Keep them carefully watered, moist but not too wet, until autumn rains return with regularity. Give each a generous layer of compost and aged manure, topped off with a blanket of mulch. If a new plant is on the tender side, one apt to winter over once established but vulnerable for the first few seasonal cycles, heap the mulch high around the crown or trunk. When you do this, add a handful of smelly, naphtha-based mothballs to discourage hungry mice from making meals off the roots, shoots, or bark.

Plant placement can affect performance greatly. Lots of subtle environmental factors are at play in most gardens. Is that suffering plant receiving too much sun or shade for its taste? Reflected light from walls, sidewalks, and swimming pools can adversely alter conditions, as can shade from neighboring trees or apartments. Is the plant's soil very dry or too damp? Hidden roots from mature trees (which might even be in another yard) may be sucking away moisture and nutrients. Alternatively, broken pipes can cause underground leaks that plants detect before we do.

Diagnosing and treating ailing plants

When you have done everything possible to please plants without apparent effect, you have two choices. If you truly desire them, you could try giving them new places that might better suit their needs. If you grow tired of the slackers, you can compost them, just like that. Not all of life's difficulties are so easily remedied, so let's enjoy those that are. Remember, it's your garden, and everything in it should earn your loving care by delighting you. If it doesn't—for any reason—out it goes.

Bellevue's Beautiful Borders

August

A spate of quixotic weather can leave many gardens looking a bit worse for wear. While heat and drought certainly take their toll, so too do tossing winds and driving rain. Combine these interesting effects and the results can be less than spectacular. If your garden is not the best ever, you are not alone in the experience.

On the other hand, unusual years can teach us a great deal about our plants. Some prove to be troopers, performing staunchly despite climatic provocation. Others may bloom out of time or sequence, creating unexpected but wonderful combinations. Though these are unlikely to recur naturally, we can draw inspiration from them, re-creating the effects with more reliably overlapping bloomers.

If you are feeling that both inspiration and a list of reliable performers would be highly welcome, it's time for a trip to Bellevue. Not to shop, mind you, but for a visit to one of the city's best-kept secrets. Just minutes from that fabled megamall is an equally fabulous garden, one that is fast developing an international reputation for excellence and originality.

Climb past the water rills that decorate the entrance to the Bellevue Botanical Garden at Wilburton Hill Park. Stroll past the Shorts Visitor Center, gaze across the wide green

170

lawn, and prepare to be amazed. Here, on a sunny slope at the edge of an elderly apple orchard, lies one of the best public display gardens in the country.

More than three hundred feet long and ninety feet wide at its deepest point, the Northwest Perennial Alliance Border overflows with summery bounty. Designed as a showcase for perennials, it presents them not in splendid isolation but in contexts created by many kinds of plants. Trees and shrubs form a woody spine for this enormous island bed, which encompasses about seventeen thousand square feet. The bays between the larger plants spill over with luscious mixtures of perennials. The whole is laced with vines, both creeping and crawling, and a huge assortment of bulbs.

The idea here is not only to show people how to create gorgeous colorist combinations with perennials, but also to demonstrate how well perennials mingle with plants of all sorts. As you follow the paths that wind along the border, color themes and sequences develop before your eyes. Walk one way and watch white, soft pinks, and lavenders warm to buttery yellows, warm reds, and plummy blues. Reverse your course and those pinks deepen to rose, gentled by creamy or silvery foliage variegation. Move past an arching wing of shrubs and suddenly you are in the torrid tropics. Volcanic reds and ember oranges sizzle alongside electric blues, their heat muted by smoldering bronze, ashen silvers, and murky purples.

Bellevue
Botanical Garden
at Wilburton Hill
Park

Created by a team of four designers and dozens of volunteers from the Northwest Perennial Alliance (a local affiliate of England's Hardy Plant Society), the border is a natural wonder. Though the scale of the border is enormous, each section contains numerous ideas that could be emulated in a modest home garden. In August the border is overflowing with summery bounty, but frequent visitors discover that it holds attractions in any season. Indeed, NPA members are constantly adding new plants to extend interest early and late.

In August, autumn cyclamen are already blooming along the

edges of the border. Everywhere, berries and hips and haws are coloring up, from the glowing reds and oranges of St. John's worts (*Hypericum* species) and shrubby viburnums to the aluminum blue beans of a lanky shrub, *Decaisnea fargesii*. Many of the border's shrubs and trees were chosen for exciting autumn foliage color as well as for interesting bark and lovely winter silhouette. In the depths of January, the border's woody bays are frothy with a wide variety of Christmas and lenten roses (*Hellebore* species). Masses of winter and early spring bulbs enliven the perennial areas, which would otherwise be very dull.

RESOURCES

FOR MORE INFORMATION, CONTACT:
THE NORTHWEST PERENNIAL ALLIANCE
PO BOX 45574
SEATTLE, WA 98145-0574

-OR-

NORTHWEST PERENNIAL ALLIANCE BORDERS AT BELLEVUE BOTANICAL GARDEN
WILBURTON HILL PARK
12001 MAIN STREET
BELLEVUE, WA 98015-4536
425/452-2750
GARDEN OPEN DAILY FROM DAWN TO DUSK, VISITOR CENTER OPEN 10 A.M. TO 5 P.M. DAILY. ADMISSION IS FREE.

Bob Lilly, one of the team of four designers, says, "My favorite thing about the border is that it exists. We did it. That's a little miracle." It is indeed inspiring to look at these ever-expanding borders and realize that they are only a few years old. Not only that, the entire effort has been sustained by volunteer labor. Bellevue's Parks Department provides vital assistance with groundskeeping and hardscape details (like fixing manifolds for the border's water supply). However, all of the planting, weeding, grooming, and maintenance of the border itself is done by members of the NPA.

Though the project has become a model for other groups and cities to emulate, it is so because so many people put so much time and effort into making the border a functional reality. "The NPA had incredible resources for a volunteer group, but we couldn't have made the project work without the cooperation of the city parks department," notes Lilly.

Most visitors are dazzled by the border's beauties, but those who want to translate them to home turf become frustrated when plants are not labeled. "The minute somebody donates the $20,000 required to have sufficiently large and immovable labels made, we'll do it," promises Lilly. "We tried labeling the first five feet of each bed, but people assumed the other plants had labels too, and just waded in looking for them, which caused incredible damage."

Plant lists are (usually) available at the visitor center, but those who really want to know the border and its plants better might consider volunteering for the NPA maintenance workshops that take place several Sundays each month. "You get to work with experienced gardeners, you learn a lot about the plants, and you learn about mixed border gardening," Lilly explains. Best of all, the border becomes your garden too.

Bats Without Belfries:
Making Bats Welcome in the Garden

 August

Although many people are interested in the idea of encouraging bats, some have reservations. Why do we need to protect bats? What are bats good for? Can bats hurt people? Are their droppings unsanitary?

Sadly, bats are becoming endangered in many places as their natural habitats are destroyed. When they try to share housing with the humans who have replaced their turf, few people are enthusiastic. We may not want an attic full of bats, but there are some good reasons to make bats welcome in our gardens, if not our belfries.

One thing bats are terrific for is catching mosquitoes. In one study, a single brown bat caught and ate more than six hundred mosquitoes in an hour. Bats also love to eat cutworm and corn borer moths. A resident family of bats can do a lot to keep the insect population in check without poisoning anything or polluting the local environment.

Here in the Northwest, where rabies is extremely rare, the odds of being harmed by a bat are minuscule. Indeed, a recent forty-year study showed that more people die each year from food poisoning at church picnics than have died in four decades from rabid bat bites (a total of ten in all of North America, including Canada—now there's a statistic for you).

In 1997, as this was being updated, the Washington Game and Wildlife Department estimated that one-tenth of one percent of the population of native bats carried rabies. We have some fifteen native species, all of which eat insects and all of which may carry rabies, but clearly, the odds are against it.

A different statistic that is sometimes quoted puts rabid bats at close to ten percent of the population. What this actually reflects is that about ten percent of the bats taken in to the health department after an encounter with humans prove to have rabies. It also means that ninety percent of them are not rabid. They may not, however, be perfectly healthy for some other reason. Most bat bites occur when people find a sick bat during daylight hours and attempt to pick it up. This is never a good idea with any wild creature exhibiting unusual behavior; if you ever do see such a thing, leave it alone and contact a zoo or wild animal preserve for assistance.

Bats
and
bat boxes

According to Liz Greenlees-Cooper, our pets' favorite vet, the best way to deal with bats in the environment is respectfully. "If one gets in the house, do not handle it directly, under any circumstances," she cautioned. "The first thing you do is open doors and windows, then get out of the way and let the bat get out."

Waving your hands or chasing with a broom are equally poor options, she notes, since both interfere with the bat's sonar directional system. If you can't get the bat out passively, Kelly MacAlister of the Washington Department of Game and Wildlife recommends donning heavy gloves and catching the bat with a thick towel. Put it in a container (a margarine tub is perfect) and take it to the health department for analysis. You can't just let it go, because bats which are found in and around human habitation are likely to be ill, or they wouldn't be there at all. The only sure way to tell whether a bat—or anything else—is rabid is by examining brain tissue, an invasive technique that is fatal to the animal. If the bat proves to be rabid, antidote shots are in order. These are expensive—running about a thousand bucks a person—so clearly it's far better to be safe than not so sure.

Rabies is very definitely a serious disease. If diagnosed before symptoms appear, that course of antidote shots can be given, nearly always successfully holding the disease at bay. Once symptoms are present, the disease is fatal. Period. Thus it makes sense not to expose ourselves unnecessarily.

Most bats are perfectly healthy, but as Greenlees-Cooper points out, "There's no point in taking chances. Lots of people are interested in bats, and that's great. Still, we have to take sensible precautions. The very first one is never to touch a bat bare-handed, under any circumstances. Recently, a child brought a bat to school, which was a public health nightmare. Bats are helpful and fascinating, but they are not show-and-tell animals." Indeed, in that case, the bat tested positive and the entire class was given the preliminary shot of the rabies series before a second test revealed that the first one had been a false positive.

Relatively few bats turn up in houses, but because those that do are often brought in by cats, Greenlees-Cooper recommends that every cat owner have outdoor cats inoculated against rabies on a regular basis. "Especially if cats are hunters: Then a simple shot can protect both the cat and the owners, should your cat ever catch a bat," she explains.

For those of us who still want to encourage bats, it's smart to locate bat boxes away from the house whenever possible. "Choose the back part of your lot, away from human traffic patterns," Greenlees-Cooper suggests. "Bats are good company in the garden, so long as we keep our distance."

As for bat droppings, or guano, being unsanitary, it's a matter of degree. According to public health statistics, both cat and dog droppings are far more dangerous than bat guano. Years ago, guano was removed from caves and sold to farmers, who prized its nutritive values as well as its tilth-building properties. Guano certainly won't hurt the garden, but if you decide to add some to the compost heap, be sure to wear gloves. A respiratory mask would be advisable if any significant amount is being moved, since any manure can carry nasty fungal spores, among other things.

Bats are undeniably messy, though, and if they are living in an inconvenient place within the garden or near the house, you may want to put up a bat box or two. Placed near their chosen area, the boxes often become the preferred habitat, though it may take a season or two for the bats to accept their new home.

Like birdhouses, bat boxes provide a comfortable, protected environment. They look a bit funny at first, however, for unlike birdhouses, bat boxes have no floor (this is because bats can't use doorways that mimic knotholes, as birds do). What's more, the interior of a bat box is divided by vertical baffles that create flat little "rooms" of various sizes, making plenty of places for a whole bat family to sleep together.

Bats don't need perches, either; they can cling to the box walls without assistance, so long as the lumber used is rough and untreated (shaggy redwood is ideal). If you decide to build a bat box, the wood you use should never be painted or stained, because paint fumes can be painfully irritating and even toxic to these little mammals. Because they are so simple, bat boxes take only a few hours to build. They make a great project for an older child, using either a kit or a pattern.

Once built and hung in place, a bat box should not be disturbed or even

RESOURCES

BAT CONSERVATION
INTERNATIONAL
PO BOX 162603
AUSTIN, TX 78716-2603
512/327-9721
WWW.BATCON.ORG

touched again once occupied, or any resident bats may be scared away. Hang bat houses twelve to fifteen feet above the ground, either on the side of a building or on a tree trunk where they will be sheltered from wind. You can group two or three boxes together or try several different locations to see which is most attractive. You will be able to tell when a box is occupied by the telltale droppings. If two years go by without bats, try moving your box to a warmer or cooler place.

Many local nurseries carry bat boxes as well as birdhouses these days. If you would like to build your own bat box, you can get a full set of plans as well as several informative pamphlets on attracting and living with bats from Bat Conservation International. (Please send a minimum donation of $7 to cover costs.)

Heat-Loving Sea Hollies

August

Staunchly upright, armed to the teeth, and boldly beautiful, sea hollies (*Eryngium* species) remind me of Scottish Highlanders zealously guarding the border. With their spiny leaves and bristling, thistle-like blossoms, these tough perennials have the feisty look of a heraldic emblem. As the common name suggests, many eryngiums are seaside plants, though others hail from mountain meadows, high plains, and open steppes. Sea hollies thrive during hot summers, handling sun and dry soils with panache. Statuesque or tiny, silvery or gray-green or metallic blue, all species have blossoms like thimbles surrounded with starry, multirayed bracts.

Remarkably long lasting in bloom, eryngiums remain decidedly ornamental for much of the garden year. Their foliage can be nearly as decorative as the flower heads. In many Mediterranean species, the stem foliage is lobed or divided and heavily spined. North and South American species look more like yuccas or agaves, with swordlike leaves edged in sharp needles.

True sea holly (*Eryngium maritimum*, to one foot) is rare in gardens, but glistening, steel blue alpine sea holly (*Eryngium alpinum*, to two feet) is better represented. This one boasts the showiest flowers in the clan. Big, bold, and arrogantly upright, they look like Elizabethan nobles, their long heads encircled in elaborate ruffs. Where many of its kin are hard on the gardener's hands, the living lace of alpine sea holly feels surprisingly soft. Ruff and all, the plant dries splendidly in winter, retaining such structural integrity that it looks more like an artifact than an elderly perennial. As the shimmering summer color drains away, leaves and stems turn a rich tobacco brown, then bleach to the silvery gray of old cedar.

Native to the European alps, this meadow dweller blooms from late summer into autumn. The species itself is less common than garden forms such as *E. a.* 'Blue Star' (almost navy blue), 'Superbum' (sapphire), and 'Amethyst' (pinky-purple). Alpine sea hollies partner well with supple, soft-edged companions such as the cream variegated maiden grass (*Miscanthus sinensis* 'Variegatus') and the fluffy, shell pink flowers of California lilac (*Ceanothus* 'Marie Simon'). Sea hollies also look smashing sandwiched between bold-leaved shrubs such as hydrangeas or purple hazel and globular ornamental onions like *Allium schubertii* or 'Globe Master', whose spherical seed heads balance the insistently linear sea hollies.

A varied group of *E. alpinum* hybrids called *E.* × *zabelii* (to two feet) were popular border plants early in the century. Though many are lost to cultivation, a handful of dazzlers remain available, all with richly tinted flowers and flaring, intricately cut bracts. Sea blue 'Donard Variety' (also sold as 'Donard Blue') and red-purple 'Violetta' are the most common. Both partner pleasantly with rugged *Rodgersia aesculifolia* and softly spilling grasses. Any of the fine-textured love grasses (*Eragrostis* species), or the rosy, gilded plumes of squirrel-tail grass, *Hordeum jubatum*, will tumble like spun silk around these structural sea hollies.

Silvery
sea hollies
for Northwest
gardens

An elegant natural hybrid, *Eryngium* × *oliverianum* (to three feet) has dark blue cones and big bracts of a lustrous, pewtery blue (which color continues well down the stems). In a memorable vignette from the late Kevin Nicolay's Seattle garden, I saw this grouped with a lovely foliage annual (*Bupleurum rotundifolium* 'Green

Gold'), a hybrid goldenrod/aster cross (× *Solidaster luteus* 'Lemore'), and blue rue (*Ruta graveolens* 'Blue Beauty'). This sea holly also makes a subtle but sumptuous companion for blue oat grass (× *Helictotrichon sempervirens*), and blue fescues such as tufty, steel gray *Festuca glauca* 'Blauglut'.

So too does the silvery giant sea holly, *Eryngium giganteum* (to four feet). Often called Miss Willmott's ghost (a suitable tribute to a rather prickly doyenne of English gardening), this short-lived perennial is generally grown from seed, since the fleshy roots are resentful of disturbance. It was said that Miss. W. scattered the seeds wherever she went, leaving hundreds of round-leaved seedlings in her wake. Since they can take several years to germinate, it's doubtful that the proliferation of giant sea holly can be credited to one woman, however doughty, yet the charming story persists.

Not surprisingly, the sea hollies are excellent seaside plants. In garden settings, they adapt well to any open, sunny, well-drained site and accept a wide range of conditions, including some truly dreadful soils. While maritime and plains species are highly tolerant of drought, others from meadows and riverbanks are often less so. Knowing the provenance of the species you want to grow will make it easier to position them appropriately. However, all deliver the best garden performance when given reasonably fertile soils and adequate moisture when in active growth.

These bolder sea hollies look best in architectural plantings, partnered with grasses or big-leaved shrubs. However, another group of sea hollies have smaller but profuse blossoms on open, airy plants. Those of Mediterranean sea holly, *E. bourgatii* (to two feet) are the color of a blue moon, finely rayed and starry. They emerge in stiff sprays above basal foliage like oiled kidskin, softly streaked with silvery veins. In twilight-colored *E. b.* 'Oxford Blue', central cones like chubby pincushions are encircled by long, slender spines. These are playfully echoed by an underplanting of a thready golden hair grass (*Deschampsia flexuosa* 'Tatra Gold'), while fluffy clouds of dwarf white sea kale (*Crambe filiformis*) offer a sensuous contrast of form and texture.

Amethyst sea holly, *Eryngium amethystinum* (to two feet), is popular in northern gardens where its tender kin freeze. Slim-rayed as pale blue stars, the clustered blossoms glimmer against lavender-blue balls of ornamental onions like *Allium christophii*. They also look great with coppery, grasslike carexes—either the militantly upright *Carex buchananii*, with its twirling brown tails, or cascades of *C. comans* 'Bronze Form'.

The tiny heads of pincushion sea holly, *Eryngium planum* (to three feet) rise like sheaves of blue buttons amid the sunny border. Native from Russia into the steppes of central Asia, this one remains dignified and decorative in lean soils and full sun, but loses its equilibrium in lusher conditions. Named forms include pale turquoise 'Blue Cap', glittering 'Blue Diamond', and icy 'Silverstone', all of which explode in little starbursts over much of the summer.

A high riser for midborder positions, *Eryngium × tripartitum* (to four feet) carries its wiry, aluminum blue flowers on leggy stems. The blue-green bracts are beautifully set off by a backdrop of dusky purple hazel and an underskirt of golden bears' breeches, *Acanthus mollis* 'Fielding's Gold'.

Similar company suits Moroccan mountain eryngo, *E. variifolium* (to two feet). (Eryngium species native to the North and South American steppes and plains are called eryngoes.) This one has a vicious grace, its bantam blue cones ruffed with spines like needles, long and glittering above heavily spiked stem foliage. The basal leaves are shaped like rounded hearts, toothed and crinkled. Where winters are mild, the basal foliage remains glossy all year, with vivid, creamy veins that stand out beautifully during the quieter months.

Only a couple of the American eryngoes are at all common in gardens. Since they are not difficult to grow, I suspect that this reflects the strength of their character, which is so pronounced as to throw off the relationship values in most perennial or mixed borders. Indeed, these are rugged individualists that do not mingle gracefully with billowing border beauties. Give them a place of their own, whether as a specimen in a sweep of gravel or in a large container by terrace or pool, and their architectural qualities shine out without dimming their neighbors.

American eryngoes can be used successfully in boldly scaled

borders if partnered with large plants with simple lines. Big grasses, tall prairie compass plant (*Sylphium* species), and bear's breeches (*Acanthus mollis*) are able companions that can match their virile potency.

North American rattlesnake master, *Eryngium yuccifolium* (three to five feet), is a dry-country plant that thrives in difficult settings. Its broad, almost succulent-looking leaves are blue-gray and edged with stubby spines. Tight sheaves of ice green flowers with diminutive, grayish bracts hug the sturdy stems, giving the plant a rather severe profile.

Too distinctive to merge comfortably into the average border, rattlesnake master looks splendid when grown in a big pot. In the garden, give it dramatic companions such as the tall, chartreuse spurge (*Euphorbia wallichii*) or black and purple *Euphorbia dulcis* 'Chameleon' and sunny golden feverfew (*Chrysanthemum parthenium* 'Aureum'). (I'm so pleased that chrysanthemum is once again a valid name for this plant.)

Wide and leathery, the long leaves of Argentinean agave eryngo, *E. agavifolium* (to three feet), bristle with spines that glow with a deadly beauty when backlit. The thick stems are studded with fog-colored or watery blue cone flowers that are more interesting than beautiful, requiring a good foil such as copper fennel or a wall hung with purple grape (*Vitis vinifera* 'Purpurea') to show them to advantage.

Most sea hollies thrive in open, sunny gardens with well-drained soil of almost any kind. Mild, organic supplements like compost, aged manure, and alfalfa pellets keep sea hollies in good health for many years. Though mature plants resent disturbance, young ones can be moved in early spring or autumn if necessary. Take a good, big rootball and they won't sulk for long in their new homes. Eryngiums also prefer mannerly companions that keep their distance; none appreciate being overhung by lush neighbors. When their modest needs are met, they provide a lengthy flow of seasonal beauties, from the time their metallic, blue-gray foliage emerges in spring to season's end, when the ornate seed heads rattle in the winter wind.

SEPTEMBER

Releasing Plant Potstickers

September

The World Series marks the time when gardeners need to winterize their pot plants. (In view of recent court rulings about the purported medicinal values of certain herbs, let me say that the following suggestions probably hold for any potted plant, whether pot or not.) Whatever their genus, recent purchases are likely to need immediate repotting into larger containers. So too are plants whose ideal garden placement has not yet been determined. Since this process may take years, the poor things can get badly potbound.

To keep them growing strongly while waiting in the wings, move them up a size or two. Anything still in a three-to-four-inch pot should go into a gallon, while single gallons can be potted into two- or five-gallon containers. Don't overdo things, though; smaller plants can struggle as much when overpotted as under.

Too much room can lead to root rots and a lack of oxygen as excess soil compacts, catching tender roots in a squeeze play. Give them a new container just a size or two larger than the last and all will be well. Those cramped roots will definitely appreciate having some toe room when the cold hits. The extra soil is still light and fluffy, letting in air and water to hungry roots, offering additional nutritional supplements, and providing some extra insulation against frost as well. (Crowded roots that are right up against the sides of the pots are very vulnerable to freezing when temperatures plummet.)

Ornamental containers also need checking. Terra-cotta pots that are not hard-fired should be trundled into the garage or basement for the winter. Such pots often chip or shatter when the water they absorb freezes. This can be fatal to pot and plant alike, for unprotected roots hate frost. Those ornamental plaques sold in garden centers are often soft-fired, and unless they are hung on walls that are protected by deep eaves, they can absorb enough moisture from the air to crumble, crack or shatter as well, so bring them in too.

Repotting is one of my favorite fall chores, because it offers such a range of skill-building challenges. It sounds simple—just slide the plant out of its old home and pop it into the new, right? In reality, plants left too long in the pot can become one with their home. The roots cling so tenaciously to the sides of the pot that they are all but impossible to dislodge.

There are several standard ways to remove such determined pot-stickers. The first technique to try is The Blade. Long-bladed kitchen knives make splendid garden tools if you can smuggle them past the cook. For deep pots, a twelve- to fourteen-inch slicer works wonders. Just slip it (wiggling helps) between the soil and the side of the pot. Work the blade all the way around the pot a couple of times. Granted, this is not markedly good for the knife, but it really sets those plants free in a hurry.

Now do The Thump. Invert the pot, using one hand to hold it and cradle the inhabitant, then give it a brisk thump or two on the bottom with the heel of your palm. If you've had any hospital experience (or watch those emergency room shows on the tube), you'll recognize this as the vegetable version of the precordial thump. Do this with vim, and quite often the initially reluctant plant will slide demurely into your hand.

Should it not do so, try The Massage (this works only with plastic pots). Place the pot on its side, bundling any loose foliage with a bit of string or netting to keep it from damage. Now press down hard on the side of the pot, putting most of your body weight on it if you are a smallish person. Roll the pot a bit and press again. Keep massaging your way around the pot until you feel the innards give a bit. Now apply The Thump again.

If it still doesn't work, don't panic; we can always resort to violence and/or destruction. Plastic pots, after all, are not irreplaceable. To perform The Recycle, you will need a pair of tin snips or sharp cutting shears (the kind they claim will cut pennies). Snip your way down the side of the pot; if this alone does not set the captive free, keep going across the bottom and up the other side. In extreme cases of pot cling, you can slice down the sides and then cut away the bottom of the pot, but leave the severed side pieces in place. To hide the evidence, just trim off the pot rim at the soil line, then simply plunge the whole mess into a huge pot or the ground. Those questing roots will find their way out of the pot without any further help from you.

Winterizing potted plants

Removing potstickers

Potting up and potting on

The trickiest potsticker situation has been solved by clever friends. Charles Price and Glenn Withey are best known as the owners of Withey/Price Landscape Design and co-designers of the Northwest Perennial Alliance Borders at the Bellevue Botanical Garden. They are also, however, highly inventive problem solvers. Recently, they found that a prized hosta had outgrown its very handsome pot. Unfortunately, the neck of this pot was smaller than its body, which makes removal of a healthy but overgrown hosta problematic.

Where destruction of the pot is not a desirable option, the usual solution (The E.R.) involves slicing the plant into manageable pieces. This can be a dicey operation in close quarters and does not necessarily produce a win-win result. To perform The Withey/Price Maneuver instead, fill a teapot with boiling water. Pour this down the inner edge of the pot, rotating slowly as you do. Soon, the outer roots of the plant will be cooked to mush, which can be scraped out like pumpkin pulp with a long-handled spoon. Most plants will not be harmed by this unceremonious treatment and can be repotted immediately. This time, however, avoid the squeeze play by choosing a large-necked pot.

But how do you repot when roots have been damaged in the process? Once a potbound plant is unstuck, then what? Whenever a plant has outgrown its container, the principles for repotting are the same. All plants need three things: nutrients, water, and air. Plants grown in pots also need enough room for their roots to spread out comfortably. As they grow, those roots will need a steady, reliable source of nourishment. A mixture of compost and aged manure makes an excellent and inexpensive potting soil. During the warm months, add a handful of slow-release fertilizer like Osmacote. During the cooler months, fresh soil will provide plenty of food.

It's fine to use commercial potting soil, but be aware that it may be too clean to be really useful without a bit of supplementation. Many commercial mixes are so thoroughly sterilized that their natural biota is dead. Just as our stomachs rely on intestinal flora to help us digest our food, plants need the enzymes and bacteria found in live soils.

In sterile soils, many nutrients remain locked up in forms that are inaccessible to growing roots. To counter this, amend commercial mixes with some homemade compost or aged manure before planting. There are a few exceptions; the Whitney Farms soil blends are very lively, for example, and can be used right out of the bag. However, if you have been puzzled by slow or uneven growth in potted plants despite using what looks like great soil mix, the problem could be soil sterility.

A second common problem arises when we use light, fine-textured soil mixtures. Those based on ground-up peat moss can dry out very quickly, especially in pots placed in sunny or windy sites. Peaty soil mix can be quite difficult to rewet unless you use hot water, which is not exactly appreciated by growing plants. Too often, such soils form a hard crust that actually repels water. As a result, the dry soil pulls away from the side of the pot. When we try to water, it just runs down the gap between pot and soil, leaving the plants as dry as ever. Bottom watering, setting plants in a deep saucer of water, will eventually cause the water to wick up into the soil, but even one session of deep drought can cause lasting harm.

If you want to lighten heavy potting mixes, it's best to leave the peat in the bog. Instead, stir in a blend of vermiculite and coarse (builder's) sand or fine grit (up to one-third by volume). This helps in two ways: The vermiculite holds water well but also releases it freely to the plants. Both vermiculite and grit create a lot of tiny air spaces in the soil. Everybody who has neglected to replant a divided perennial in time knows that too much air can kill roots. (If you haven't yet realized this, try leaving a bare-root plant out in the open for a few days. You can almost watch the roots shrivel, in or out of direct sun.)

Most gardeners also know that excessively loose soil can leave big air pockets that kill roots. However, soils that are too fine or too heavy can become tightly compacted. No air at all leads to anaerobic situations, which encourage molds and rots rather than healthy roots. In short, we want to offer our potted plants open-textured soils that accept moisture readily but drain well and also deliver a mild but steady supply of nutrients to hungry roots.

Whether plants are bound for the border or for another pot, tightly compacted rootballs should be teased loose before replanting. Really rootbound plants can require fairly rough handling to open out the roots. Experienced gardeners know that the flattened mats of roots that lined the sides of the old pot need to be fluffed, scuffed, or even torn a bit before replanting. It may look like plant torture, but the result is as refreshing to bound roots as the release to the spirit when we burst past our own outgrown limitations.

Must pots be cleaned before reuse? Well, yes and no. If the plant was sickly or died of mysterious causes, if the soil was threaded with mold or crusted with mineral deposits, yes. Wash such pots with warm water with a bit of bleach added, then let them air dry thoroughly before reuse. If the plants were healthy and their soil looks and smells good, the pots can be pressed into service immediately. Give them a rinse if you like.

Clay pots that have white mineral stains, moss, or the green slime that is the precursor of moss on them can also be cleaned, but they don't really need to be. Indeed, some gardeners paint terra-cotta pots with buttermilk to promote this green haze, which makes them appear comfortably ancient. (It's also very English looking.)

Finally, can old potting soil be reused? This is almost never worthwhile. Drenched by so many waterings, potting soil becomes exhausted of nutrients. Soil that still feels and smells good can be mixed with grit and used to fill the bottom third of a huge pot. Otherwise, recycle it through the compost heap, where it will be restored to health and tilth.

Gardening with Abandon

 September

A few years ago, I noticed that a yard I pass almost daily was starting to sprout a garden. The house is a very ordinary one, tucked among other suburban homes on a quiet side street. The lot is small and had previously been practically empty. That summer, however, the modest front yard was awash in flowers all summer long. The next year, a flood of flowers encircled the house and spilled around the feet of the garage.

It was an astonishing sight, this garden. Throughout its neighborhood, the yards are mostly neat but nondescript. Suddenly, this bland uniformity was interrupted by an ebullience of roses, a wall of towering mallows, a sea of sunflowers. Despite the summer's mixture of heat and drought, wind and hard rain, the garden had bloomed nonstop since April. As September opened, it showed no signs of slacking.

It's always a pleasure to watch the fruits of floral passion develop, and I watched this little garden's progress with great interest. I was delighted, therefore, to be invited to a garden party there, a celebration of summer and flowers. Our hostess, Teri Cole, had filled the yard with flowery sofas and overstuffed chairs, creating soft places to sit and admire her handiwork. Little tables were clustered about so that people could eat cozily together. As twilight gathered, candles flickered everywhere, their gentle light awakening sunset colors in the hundreds of roses.

All evening, the guests wandered through the garden, first by daylight, then in the deepening dusk. The guests were a garden in themselves—all women, each as dazzling as the next, dressed for fun and flourish, enjoying themselves and each other. The evening's easy camaraderies and affectionate interplay expressed an appreciation of the floral lushness of womanity.

The garden, too, was all about abundance. Each bed was fuller than the last, foaming with flowers of all kinds. By day, the fiery-colored flowers drew the eye, their leaping reds and oranges and golds as cheerful as a Mexican open-air market. As the light drained away, the paler colors predominated. Now white flowers, and creams and gentle yellows, glowed, while blues and hazy lavenders phosphoresced in the buttery moonlight. The warm air was velvety with scents, both herbal and floral.

Simple in design and relying heavily on old-fashioned cottage garden plants, the garden created an impression of almost incredible abundance. Herbs and vegetables mingled comfortably with annuals and perennials. Sweet-scented honeysuckle twined between shrubs and scrambled up the fence. Living walls of tall, shrublike perennial mallow, *Lavatera thuringiaca* 'Barnsley', were smothered with hundreds of pastel pink flowers like crepe paper hollyhocks.

Underfoot, the ground was carpeted with masses of petunias and pansies, sheets of salmon pink twinspur (*Diascia*), and fragrant white sweet woodruff. Roses were everywhere, lining the paths and tumbling out of beds. Young climbing roses were being trained to clamber up stout poles (left over from a vigorous apple-pruning session) in the backyard. Here, a rustic arbor was taking shape under Cole's capable hands. Soon, it would be roofed with roses and probably decked with clematis and jasmine as well.

What makes this happen? Why are some people incredibly successful gardeners, often despite difficult settings? Why are some people naturals even when inexperienced, while others can study for years without enjoying the same degree of effortless success? How can some gardens flourish overnight, transforming their very surroundings, as this one so magically does? Anybody who walks city streets seeking out small gardens sees this phenomenon again and again. One day, a little lot is barren and unprepossessing. The house changes hands, and all of a sudden a garden sprouts into being with the vigor of a fairy tale beanstalk. It is often suggested that virgin soil or the infatuated attention of the new gardener is responsible for beginner's luck. Perhaps optimism, as yet untinged by experience, influences plants to grow abundantly.

I believe that the real difference lies in the gardener. In this example, the gardener has abandoned herself to the garden. She allows her delight in it to fill her life as well as her yard. The rush of flowers sweeps her away daily in glorious, passionate embrace. As a result, she herself is a garden, a veritable bower of blossom for her family and friends. Her garden reaches even further,

Abundant
gardens

touching the lives of everybody who walks or even drives by. It is impossible to pass such an explosively joyful place without a smile and an almost unconscious relaxation of tension. "Oh, right," we think; "all's right with the world. I almost forgot."

I was recently introduced to a concept that psychologists call "flow." This is the state of well-being in which we feel deeply at ease, when time stops for us. When we do things that allow us to experience flow, we don't want to be doing anything else. In a recent book called *The Optimistic Child* (Houghton Mifflin, 1995), the author, Martin Seligman, says that "(Flow) is one of the highest states of positive emotion, a state that makes life worth living."

It comes, he says, when we are doing what we truly love to do. For gardeners, flow may occur during a meditative weeding session. It can happen as we plan a new bed or border or tend a mature one. We also have the unexpected gift of sharing our own flow times with others. Being in Teri's delicious garden clearly created feelings of flow in her guests as well as in herself. (This was made especially obvious when most of us refused to go home at a reasonable hour. The moon was full, so were we, and the party rolled on and on . . .)

Gardens that work like this are gardens whose joyful exuberance is reflected in the hearts of the gardeners. Which came first is hard to say, but those who permit floral alchemy to alter their souls will find similar riches whenever they open the soil and set plants.

Prepare for Glory

September

As school doors reopen to swallow up the children, the garden suddenly becomes far quieter. As if realizing it was no longer needed, summer seems to slip away with the kids. Though the fading of summer is always sad and the house seems very empty (and incredibly quiet), the crisp touch of fall in the air lifts the gardener's spirits. Overnight, the seasonal tide has turned. A few days ago, it was too hot and dry to plant new acquisitions or disturb established plantings. Today, though the autumn equinox is still several weeks away, it's time.

In summer, we can fully savor the garden, reveling in its overflowing bounty. Indeed, we'd better, for interference can lead to more harm than good. We can water and weed a bit, but once the foliar tapestry has knit together, the borders are far too full to work in without damage. What's a gardener to do? The philosophical retreat to the hammock or chaise lounge and determine to enjoy themselves thoroughly. We gaze admiringly at bed and border, watching the pageant of color come and go, taking in details and studying the altering balance between flower and foliage.

Until the weather breaks, all this analysis remains academic. In September, however, those summer observations can be acted upon. However much we may like summery lounging, this is the moment gardeners secretly long for. Even those who don't keep garden journals have no hesitation about what to do first. I remember when my oldest son was a baby just learning to crawl. He seemed so absorbed in mastering the movement that I didn't realize it was about something quite different. The minute he became mobile, he headed straight for the cat food dish, then to an especially intriguing electrical socket. Those spots had clearly been calling him, just as the waiting garden, tantalizingly out of reach, calls to us.

Now we sail joyfully in, eager to correct all those annoying little mistakes that revealed themselves over the summer. Even when deeply relaxed, gardeners can never quite overlook their garden's faults. The loving but critical eye of the inner gardener never goes off duty. Now it leads to a delicious flurry of fussing, with keenly appreciated results.

The first day of renewed garden activity has a merry ebullience about it, like any long-awaited pleasure. Early autumn is a blissful time to be a gardener. The weather may be changing, but there are still dozens of golden days when both air and soil are bathwater warm. Many summer bloomers are still looking great, and a good few are just hitting their stride. Fall planting beats spring chores hollow. Comfortable, dry, surrounded by beauty, we work in happy concentration. Early bloomers can be lifted and moved or divided and reset. Plants that lost their luster too soon can be moved farther back in the border or given new frontal companions that will rise to hide their shame next season.

This is an excellent time to tease out the grass roots that invariably infiltrate iris clumps. Old clumps bloom far better when broken up periodically, for left untouched they often grow woody and sparse or go entirely to leaf. Big clumps of Siberian or bearded iris may demand serious division. Use a sturdy, square-tined garden fork to pry out the clumps—really big ones may require two forks and two people to lift. If the plants are too overgrown to be pulled apart by hand, chop them in sections with a small ax or slice them with a sharp-bladed shovel. Toss any old, woody roots on the compost heap. Pull or cut big chunks into smaller crowns with two or three clusters of leaves on each. Set these in renewed soil, arranging them in triangles or wedges, with each piece facing the same direction. Next summer, each group will fatten up nicely, full of bloom and healthy foliage. If you have too many, pot them up for donation to the upcoming arboretum plant sale, or donate them to a neighborhood church or nursing home.

Bulb shipments start to arrive, just in time for the cooler weather. Planting bulbs is another great fall delight, for it is such a hopeful activity. As we tuck them in place, we see not just the aging borders of fall but the bright ones of springs yet unborn. If you happened to make notes in spring about where you wanted to see these bulbs blossom, they will assist this process enormously. It can be tricky to match early bloomers to their companions when both are sleeping. Maps marked with key plantings, real and projected, are the best memory jogger, but if you are working blind, the best thing to do is to work slowly. Dig in haste, repent at leisure. Otherwise, you will infallibly spear some precious, long-established bulb or dormant early perennial through the heart. Approach fall bulb planting with the cautious respect of an archaeologist, patiently unearthing fragments of a lost civilization inch by careful inch. You may be amazed by the artifacts you turn up, and the planting experience will definitely be less fraught with grief.

Fall planting

Bulb planting

Breaking up iris clumps

Editing beds and borders

Perhaps the most satisfying fall project is refinement of existing combinations, those that almost but don't quite work. Often, simply prinking a bit makes a huge difference. Move those plants a bit closer, or set them a shade farther apart, and the entire relationship is redefined. When each plant is used well, it contributes with its whole self—form and texture, leaf shape and color—instead of making a shapeless lump of flowers. Architectural planting relies on calling out the sculptural qualities inherent in each plant, not only on its fleeting flowers. Compositions based on the plant as a whole are more visually satisfying in and out of bloom than merely floral combinations.

September is also a rewarding time to wander through the garden, taking notes and recording your impressions. Which combinations please you, and why? Which fail, and why? Great color combinations may look awful once the flowers have faded, leaving a leafy mess that looks mushy and graceless. Again, the strongest, longest-lasting combinations are generally those that emphasize the essential structure of each plant. A feathery, silken little grass like dainty *Stipa tenuissima* makes a sloppy mess if jumbled amid too many little-leaved companions. However, it makes a smashing little fountain of green and gold when sandwiched between the rosy broccoli of upright *Sedum* 'Autumn Joy' and the broad, mahogany leaves of a dusky coral bell like *Heuchera* 'Chocolate Ruffles'.

When designers talk about using plants in sweeps and masses, what they are getting at is that unless we use enough of each plant, smaller ones won't read effectively. Larger plants may indeed succeed as singletons, especially in little gardens where sweeps are out of scale with the setting. In any situation, however, the question is one of visual balance. This is the time to mess around with our plants, rearranging them in larger or smaller groups to find the most satisfying quantity of each. Because plants are alive, garden balance is dynamic. It changes from year to year, season to season. This requires us to keep editing, reviewing the beds and borders for shifts and changes that may need intervention. In fall, we can play with our plants until we have them in utterly pleasing relationships. If something movable doesn't look quite right, forget about taking notes. Put down your pen and pick up a shovel. This is the time!

Editing the Woods

 September

Here in the Northwest, many gardeners are faced with the challenge of creating attractive transitions between their gardens and the towering native trees around them. Like so many others, my new garden is surrounded on two sides by what passes for woods these days—the forty-or-so-foot-wide greenbelt left by law between adjoining rural and suburban properties.

The little house sits on a knoll above a sloping meadow that ends in a small stream. Thickly lined with salmonberry, native red-twigged dogwoods, and alder seedlings, the stream and its boggy surroundings meld perfectly into the real woods behind them. The addition of a few ornamental dogwoods with brilliant green or gold twigs, along with a couple of river birches, has caused the once degraded wetlands to merge happily with both meadow and garden. Repeating the plantings nearer to the house reinforces the visual relationship between the two areas.

The meadow, too, is not a real meadow but a new one, scraped out of a ragged patch of alder and scotch broom. Both would like to come back, accompanied by stinging nettles and those lusty Himalayan blackberries brought so thoughtfully to us by Luther Burbank, who felt our creeping

199

native blackberry lacked vigor. An infusion of this hearty Himalayan would do wonders, he thought, and so we see. It is indeed wonderful in the old sense what they can do to a pasture (or to your arm), but in gardener's terms it was a dubious achievement. Thanks, Luther, but no thanks. Anyway, editing here consists of mowing the meadow three or four times a year, just to keep the blackberries, broom, and nettles at bay. (An occasional hand weeding with a mattock also helps a great deal.)

The southern and western sides of the house face the meadow and are relatively open to sun and the pretty view. To unify the shady, woodsy sides and the sunnier ones, the entire house is encircled by deep beds that swing around and overlap with graveled paths that terrace the sloping hillside. East and west, neighboring homes are screened from view by broad berms. These make large, long beds filled with small trees and shrubs to divide the garden from the neighbors' yards. These woody barriers act as living walls, offering a succession of flowers and fruit as well as a fascinating diversity of foliage.

So far, so good. To the east and north, however, the greenbelts create a very different environment. Immediately behind the little cottage, a jumble of huge old cedars, hemlocks, and firs rises up abruptly. The garden's eastern edge is marked by an enormous old vine maple, its bark crusted with moss, its gnarled toes curling lumpily into the earth. This great matriarch demanded respectful treatment in her own right, and has a further value as a piece of living sculpture. However, that grandiosity of scale made our new plantings look somewhat pathetic when juxtaposed with the maple's majestic bulk. Here, we needed to spring for some good-sized evergreen shrubs that would create convincing visual transitions between garden and woods.

The other parts of the garden came together with relative ease, their design and planting guided by function. In most cases, this meant combining privacy screening with a good flow of seasonal color. Where seating areas were planned, the plants were also chosen to deliver an ongoing sequence of fragrant flowers all year round. The shady beds on the north and east sides of the house were planted with a mixture of shrubs and perennials similar to those in the sunnier, open beds, but their color schemes are muted rather than vivid. Both flowers and variegated foliages are in shades of cream or white, soft yellows and chartreuse. This brightens the shaded area without startling the eye, and makes the transition to native plantings unobtrusive.

The beds that edge the woods were the last to be planted. Before they were even shaped, I edited the woods themselves. The first step in grooming transitional woodlands is to remove the litter of broken branches from the forest floor. This takes very little time yet rewards the eye immediately. With the worst clutter gone, the intrinsic lines of the native plantings reveal themselves with increased drama. Any long-rotted logs and stumps can be left in place, especially those that are shaggy with moss or crusted with lichens. Sometimes fascinating patterns of crisscrossed logs develop, making a mossy mosaic for your garden floor. Their subtle shapes and textures can direct the placement of any plants you may decide to add, but what the woods offer up is often beautiful enough as is that the scene doesn't require any further embellishment.

Creating attractive transitions between the garden and the woods

Next, take your clippers and wade in there. Take a good look at all existing native evergreen shrubs, which will probably include huckleberry, salal, and Oregon grape. Start by grooming them lightly, clipping away anything that's dead or broken. Where plants have been damaged by builders or wandering deer, snip them back to handsome, healthy new growth, keeping the overall shape of the shrub intact whenever possible. Nearly all of our native shrubs respond nicely to careful pruning, putting on glossy new shoots in short order. Treasures like rotting old stumps trimmed with sword ferns or lacy huckleberries will become winter focal points in these shady havens, so clean them up with care, leaving mushrooms and mosses and whatnot, and removing only stuff that distracts from their charms.

Sword ferns are ubiquitous, so it's lucky they are so beautiful. In order to show that beauty to the wondering world, we need to get rid of past glory in the shape of rusting old fronds that clutter the base of the crowns. I also take off any upright fronds that are burned by frost, so that only fresh green remains. If you have a lot of ferns to tidy, do it wholesale and whack the entire lot to the ground. This looks brutal at first, but the ferns will bounce back in no time, their purity of line unsullied by tatty leftovers. While you're at it, take time to pick up any other old leaves and sticks and so on that reduce the overall good looks of the setting. Be sure not to get too carried away, though; this is not a job for the Dustbuster. The woodsy garden needs all of that rich, crumbly forest duff to be left in place. It's better than any compost we could buy and will replenish the roots of shy wildlings like trilliums and vanilla leaf.

You can treat deciduous shrubs like salmonberry, cream bush, and Indian plum in the same manner, looking first, and then removing only that which detracts from the overall appeal of the plant. Often these things sow themselves into thickets that need thinning if any are to grow up properly. Here, thin to reveal shape, and leave enough elbow room for each to develop its own distinctive form. The last thing to do is work upward, reaching up and breaking off as many dead lower limbs from the mature trees as you can reach. If possible, get a ladder and saw them off close to the trunks, so you leave smooth columns rather than raggedy ones.

Step back from your labors and prepare to be amazed. What you are looking at is a genuinely natural garden. Elegant and understated, natural gardens are the despair of Zen practitioners, who strive to achieve that same effortless clarity of line and form all their working days. Where gaps or holes need filling, try inserting graceful laceleaf maples, azaleas, dogwoods, or similarly airy, shapely plants.

To make convincing transitions to more contrived beds, we can combine natives with their imported relatives. Let native winter currant, rosy *Ribes sanguineum*, arch over the path, and tuck some of the wonderful Chinese ribes with huge or long-fingered foliage into the background for contrast of form and flower. Underplant your transitional areas with evergreen Oregon shamrock, *Oxalis oregana*, either with creamy flowers or the rosy 'Winter Form', whose blossoms are bright pink and whose fluttering leaves are backed with burgundy. Both evergreen and deciduous inside-out flower (*Vancouveria* species) will creep in ruffled carpets over forest and garden floor alike. Evergreen *V. planipetala* has glossy, duck-footed little leaves and fluttering white flowers, smaller than those of deciduous *V. hexandra*. Prettiest of all is the Oregonian *V. chrysantha*, a lustrous evergreen with sunny yellow flowers. It grows more slowly than the others and is an ideal ground cover to let loose amongst treasures that more vigorous carpets might swamp.

This idea of blending natives with allies and relatives can be carried on in all directions and is great fun. We can blend all sorts of exotic cousins in with our native maidenhair, lady, and sword ferns. Native Oregon grape (*Mahonia aquifolium*) has several beautiful relatives, such as Chinese *M. bealei*, with larger leaves and showier flowers. Native heucheras and tiarellas have hundreds of fine-looking kin to commingle with native and imported grasses, reeds, and rushes. Skunk cabbage, eastern and western, fits comfortably with veratrums from here and elsewhere.

Once your woods are tidied up, it becomes easy to see where new plants may be added without disrupting the natural, inherent garden. The respectful process of editing is both less destructive and more revealing than the average remodel, which begins in removal and often ends in tears. Take your time, move slowly, and let the plants themselves tell you how to weave those all-important transitions. The result will be richer, deeper, and more magical than anything that happens when we simply try to impose our preconceived concepts on a space that is far from empty.

OCTOBER

Going with the Glow

 October

October brings a haze of heat to the borders, not only from late sunshine (or so we hope), but from blazing leaves. The color builds along the roadside as well as in the garden. Vine maples bloom into billows of brilliant reds and coppery oranges, especially glorious when framed against murky firs or purple-leaved plums. Along the city streets, slim sweet-gums (*Liquidambar*) leap skyward like flaming rockets, scattering their bright leaves like so many sparks. In abandoned lots, feathery, exotic-looking sumacs (*Rhus*) exchange their normal bottle green for deep, hot hues that give them the look of ferns at a costume party.

In the garden, color pours in from all sides. Many ornamental dogwoods color splendidly, some in shocking pink and saturated raspberry, others in cranberry, salmon, and peach. The broad, rounded foliage of witch hazels (*Hamamelis*) and their bottle-brush cousin, *Fothergilla gardenii*, have been licked with a searing brush, their fiery colors intensified by cascades of lavender-blue *Aster × frikartii* 'Wonder of Stafa' and the bluer 'Monch'.

One of my favorite vines, *Mina lobata*, has maple-like leaves and long sprays of tubular flowers that deepen in color as they move up the glossy black stem, changing from cream to yellow to orange to vivid red. Still smothered under masses of bloom, the vine winds through a potted red banana tree, enlivening its dusky leaves with her gay color run. The banana really needs to come inside for the winter, as do its neighbors, a large, copper-red New Zealand flax (*Phormium tenax*) and a *Brugmansia* 'Charles Grimaldi', a small tree with enormous leaves and flared, trumpeting orange sherbet flowers eight inches long.

These tender creatures live in large pots, which, though heavy, are easy to move with the help of a hand truck. The difficulty lies in tearing away the soft web of flowers and foliage that laces these free-standing plants together. That busy *Mina* (who lives in the banana pot) throws her showy shawl around everybody's shoulders, and it takes a harder heart than mine to rip it away. I really must do it, though, for if taken indoors before a biting frost, *Mina* herself may flower through the winter for me, keeping company with the dangling bells of datura. Related to dahlias, it has a plump storage root that melts to mush at the least touch of frost, but putts along just fine at moderate indoor temperatures. True, she is quite prone to spider mites and aphid infections inside (as are the flax and the brugmansia), but frequent spraying with a water mister helps a good deal.

Were that coppery phormium planted in the ground, it would very likely prove hardy, especially if the winter is mild. Darker green forms are completely hardy well into Cascadia, and even the colorful, more tender pink and red forms can take cold in stride once established. However, pot-grown specimens are often hammered by the cold. Though they usually recover, it takes so long for them to regain their looks that the plants are essentially worthless for most of the year. In cold, damp, or windy gardens, it's a good idea to keep borderline hardy plants of this sort in pots so they can spend the winter safely inside.

Lots of solidly hardy plants color attractively in October, when autumn arrives in earnest. Not only do the well-known shrubs and trees blaze away, but plenty of border foliage plants also turn. Most of them boast pretty if less incendiary tints, usually clear gold, soft bronze, and buttery yellows. Some of the tall Siberian iris gild nicely, as do several huge old hostas. The long-fingered rodgersias and big *Astilboides tabularis* (formerly *Rodgersia tabularis*), round as a dinner plate, become ruddy and bronzed, like sailors long at sea. A few perennials take on warmer tints, like the lesser leadwort, *Ceratostigma plumbaginoides*, a loose-textured ground cover that makes a splendid cover for small bulbs. Dormant in spring, it becomes an open weaver in summer, hiding fading foliage nicely. In the fall, its small, tidy leaves turn richly red, setting off its gentian-blue flowers to perfection.

The happy Himalayan scrambler, *Polygonum affine* 'Dimity', is a screamer too, turning searing red in fall. This pleasant little edger makes an impenetrable carpet of tidy leaves and knotted stems, and though only semievergreen, it keeps weeds at bay by presenting a solid front to intruders.

That persistent wildling, *Geranium robertianum*, is a pest in the garden but a blessing in the wild border, where it suppresses worse weeds with a great goodwill. In October, this weedy herb truly earns its place. Although its tiny, dirty-pink flowers are worthless, its leaves are lovely, lobed and lacy as big snowflakes. They turn blood red in the fall, as translucent and glowing as the sheaves of blood grass (*Imperata cylindrica* 'Rubra') nearby. Unfortunately, its rampant ways have earned it a slot on the weed busters' Least Wanted list. The King County Noxious Weed Control Program considers herb Robert a serious pest and hopes to convince gardeners to destroy any plants that turn up in our gardens. Ever since purple loosestrife and English ivy taught us what determined interlopers can do, wildlife protection service people have stayed alert to possible dangers. Nobody was too concerned about herb Robert so long as it confined itself to our gardens. No formal complaints were filed until it started turning up along public trails in protected wilderness areas, probably sneaking in on hikers' shoes. These days, our rule of thumb must be, When in doubt, weed it out.

Autumn color

Shrubs tend to stay put, and many of the early bloomers take on tender tints in fall, from lilacs to hydrangeas, whose leaves turn a sandy beige that sets off the faded foam of their flowers with romantic delicacy. A compact (two to three feet), shrubby St. John's wort, *Hypericum androsaemum* 'Albury Purple', carries wine purple new leaves backed in clear burgundy, then frosted with silvery pink. In fall, the old leaves deepen to red and purple edged in black, looking most dapper when interset with a form of the green-and-purple parrot's head lily (*Alstroemeria psittacina*) called 'Variegata', which has a neat white border to its slim, whorling leaves.

Common forsythias can be surprisingly handsome in fall, aglow with dark reds and ember oranges. So can many spiraeas, from old-fashioned bridal wreath (*Spiraea × vanhouttei*) to the newest border beauty, tiny little 'Magic Carpet'. This is a sport of the fabulous *S. japonica* 'Goldflame', a colorist's dream whose spring foliage starts off a strong, tawny bronze, softening to lemony chartreuse in summer, then heating up to desert sunset colors in fall. 'Magic Carpet' is smaller (under a foot tall) and similarly colorful, with even stronger autumn foliage. By October, they have all turned a lovely pumpkin color, contrasting deliciously with a shimmering brown grass, *Carex comans* 'Bronze Form', and masses of russet chrysanthemums.

All this belated glory, glowing or muted, interferes seriously with a big fall cleanup. When you begin stretching out the garden year, endings and beginnings become blurry. When does it stop? Well, it never really has to stop at all. Instead of tearing into the borders, I tidy lightly but often. This keeps those late-season vignettes looking clean-edged and keeps the weeds at bay. In a new garden like mine, a great deal of planting and rearranging can go on without major disturbance. In mature gardens, some interference is unavoidable, yet working with light hands keeps it to a minimum, allowing us to enjoy the garden's dimming delights for as long as possible.

Bulbs and Bargains

 October

There is an exciting sense of potential energy about fall
planting. Those dry, lumpy bulbs we plug in muddily as tired
leaves tumble seem such unlikely packages for the bright
flowers of spring, yet we know they will deliver unstintingly.
Just as that implicit promise refreshes the spirit, the eye is
renewed by viewing the garden from our knees.

This novel perspective allows us to see plants and their
relationships in a new light. When we are weeding or grooming, we are down there on business. Planting bulbs, we are
just visiting. As we move carefully through the beds and borders, our passage releases dozens of scents, both pungent
and perfumed. Flowers and foliage alike are at eye level,
where we can appreciate subtle details of coloration and texture usually lost to distance.

Some garden chores don't allow for the dreamy, reflective
spirit in which we plant bulbs. Hurried and purposeful,
planting and transplanting have the urgency of life-or-death
situations. It's okay to drift off in reverie when planting
bulbs, for unlike newly dug perennials, bulbs aren't going to
dry out while they wait for us to come back on task. Bulbs
don't mind at all if we drift off into the collective, losing our
small selves in the bigness of the garden as a whole.

Sit quietly for long enough and the secret life of the garden makes itself known. Garter snakes glide silently by, seeking slugs. Bugs clamber up stems. Spiders spin webs and wait for a careless visitor to drop in. Busy ants carry home food for winter stores. Butterflies and bees collect nectar. Birds flutter down to hunt worms and seeds. Nodding flowers lift their heads to the warming sun. Closed buds open and faded blossoms shatter. Tucked in intimate embrace, we enter into the communal life of the garden.

Golden autumn days are perfect for planting all sorts of things—not only bulbs, but the seeds of ideas and new visions. The slow, meditative work allows thought to flow freely, unchanneled in the usual narrow tunnels that rush to assigned destinations. In more directly practical terms, it's also an ideal time to plant early- and summer-flowering perennials, as well as most vines, shrubs, and trees. Even in chilly years, when summer seems to have flown away early, the soil should remain warm enough through November to encourage a good deal of root growth before winter closes in. Most years, it's as soothing as a baby's bathwater, wrist warm and softly enveloping, a perfect environment for questing young roots.

October is also an optimal time to add fall color to the garden. If summery combinations are looking weary, restimulation with a refreshing influx of later bloomers will pay off handsomely. Nursery hopping in the fall is a lot of fun, because there's so little gap between finding lovely new plants and seeing how they'll look in our gardens. In spring, we are buying potential. In the fall, we are buying performance.

Nursery cruising is especially rewarding when we remember to look past the usual. While there's nothing wrong with loading up on pungent chrysanthemums and bright-faced winter pansies (who can resist?), take time to wander through the other departments as well. Autumn beauties like sumacs and maples are just beginning to blaze. Viburnums and dogwoods are still smoldering, with weeks of buildup to come before they burst into flame. Less obvious plants may color gorgeously as well. The foliage of certain peonies turns apricot and peach, looking smashing with upright sheaves of grassy, red-gold *Carex buchananii* and orange-flowered *Agastache barberi* 'Firebird'.

Azaleas, too, often take on hot tints that give them a second season of dramatic beauty.

Though it's immediately pleasurable to buy plants in full fig, remember to keep your eyes open for bargains that may not be displaying any particular charms at the moment. Perennials of all sorts benefit from fall planting, and a shabby-looking spring bloomer tucked in now will bloom its socks off come April. Autumn is the sensible time to stock up on garden staples, basics that blend with everything (especially those on sale). Purple sage and blue rue, gilded grasses and silvery artemisias are all masterful mixers that reconcile warring colors or perk up pokey ones.

Planting bulbs and later bloomers

Stocking up on garden staples

Inspiration from Asian gardens

Sometimes we need mental refreshment as much as our gardens. English models for autumn gardens are much of a muchness: either nonexistent or heavily dependent on the fading charms of slumping maturity. Those who feel, after a long, hard year of garden work, that they have earned the right to expect more from the garden—say, a bit of crispness and even some showboat dazzlement—will do well to seek inspiration elsewhere. A leisurely, strolling visit to the Japanese Garden at Seattle's Washington Park Arboretum and the nearby Kubota Gardens will leave you with plenty of ideas.

Gardeners in San Francisco or Portland or Victoria or Vancouver also have excellent alternatives to those English models, which are well worth exploring in autumn. At any time of year, Asian gardens offer quite as many lessons to the garden maker as English gardens do, though perhaps less directly. For starters, in Asian gardening traditions, plants are often treated as sculptural objects, not just as blobs and smears of seasonal color. There is also an emphasis on revealing the essential qualities of the whole plant. Placed with respect, trees and shrubs gain dignity. When plants of any kind are allowed ample room to develop and display their essential character, it blossoms forth, just as people (or animals) blossom when they are supported and appreciated for who they really are.

In utterly practical terms, Asian garden traditions tend to treat autumn and winter as prime time in the garden. Scenes and vignettes are based on how the garden looks in any or every season. Even details like how the rain will look and sound when dripping from a gutter are incorporated into the overall garden design. Slow visits, repeated often, allow us to absorb such quiet, understated specifics.

> RESOURCES
>
> JAPANESE GARDEN
> WASHINGTON PARK ARBORETUM
> 1501 LAKE WASHINGTON
> BOULEVARD EAST
> SEATTLE, WA
> CALL 206/684-4725 FOR HOURS.
>
> KUBOTA GARDENS
> FOR VISITING INFORMATION,
> CALL 206/684-4584.
> FOR A TAPED ANNOUNCEMENT
> OF GARDEN EVENTS, CALL
> THE KUBOTA FOUNDATION,
> 206/725-5060.

Simply by admiring, letting our eyes drink in details and relationships between plants and objects, we allow the underlying principles to reveal themselves. We won't all want to adopt them wholesale, but here in the Northwest, the sensibility that refines Asian gardens to high art permeates our aesthetic awareness, whether we know it or not. It's part of what sets our sculptural, more architectural styles apart from typical color-mush, and part of what helps us to integrate objects into our garden settings with unusual savvy and style. Going back to take a good look at the subtle source for this flair and fun can be startling, but it also helps to stimulate new ways to see, and new ways to plant, and nothing will more enrich both us and our gardens.

Autumn Brilliance

October

As autumn advances, the last of summery leftovers fade, leaving the field to true fall flowers. Asters and chrysanthemums are perhaps the best known of these, for excellent reasons, since both are willing, hard working, and all but tireless performers that adapt readily to a wide mix of conditions. Asters have the alphabetical lead, if no deeper superiority, and make a logical starting point for the leap into autumnal bloom.

The most famous aster of the century must be *Aster* × *frikartii*, celebrated almost universally as an unstoppable performer and a high starter on many a list of all-time best border plants. A lusty four- to five-footer, this indefatigable plant pours out generous cascades of lavender blue daisies from late summer until hard frost. Its sibling hybrids, the darker blue 'Monch', paler 'Wonder of Stafa', and Wedgewood blue 'Jungfrau', are harder to find but just as gardenworthy here in the Northwest. Elsewhere, hot nights can dampen their ardor and slow flower production to a trickle after Labor Day.

All of these asters have similarly smoky colors that contrast pleasingly with the richer purples of smoke bush *Cotinus coggygria* 'Velvet Cloak') and that almost relentless long bloomer, *Verbena* 'Homestead Purple'. This colorful sprawler is still going strong in October, after four months of bloom, at least in gardens that please it. Open, sunny settings with quick-draining soils seem to be the best for keeping 'Homestead Purple' contented. Soggy clay soils send it homeward to eternal rest in a heartbeat, and in almost any setting, it seems to resent overly close company. To feel really at home, it seems to need plenty of elbow room. In some gardens, especially shady ones with heavy soils, slugs won't let it out of the ground. You may think you have lost your plants to the winter, but if you are really observant in early spring, you may see shoot after shoot struggle to make it past the ever-vigilant slime bags. A bit of bait, early in the year, might make it a more permanent resident in such gardens.

The New England asters, which are legion, provide a range of colors, from white to hot pink, but my favorites are always smudgy blue and murky purples. Like the frikart asters, these quietly sumptuous creatures combine beautifully with the warm pinks of barberry, *Berberis thunbergii* 'Rose Glow', the rose and purple *Sedum* 'Vera Jameson', and the salmon-rose blossoms of *Potentilla nepalensis* 'Miss Willmott'. All of these are still in good looks, especially from a distance. Being a bit nearsighted is a great advantage to gardeners, for it veils even a slight distance in kindly mystery. When I look at my barberry, I see only its truly rosy glow, not the gaps left by its unleafing. Vera is still a cumulus cloud of sunset rose and purple, and Miss Willmott's strawberry blossoms are unmarred by age. My new bifocals are terrific in some situations, but I never wear them in the garden, where I prefer to see the world in a delicate, almost numinous haze.

In my new garden, a shady woodland path is lined with the creamy foam of eastern wood aster, the native *Aster divaricatus*. The straight species blooms in lax tumbles, its tiny, off-white flowers bending the wiry black stems with the sheer weight of their vast numbers. Tolerant of constant shade and summer-dry soils, this finely constructed aster accommodates well to our wet winters and springs, clumping up quickly and flowering for several months from midsummer well into fall. My wood asters alternate handsomely with shaggy clumps of gold-striped water grass (*Hakonechloa macra* 'Aureola') and natty clusters of black mondo grass, *Ophiopogon planiscapus* 'Nigrescens'. Had I realized how wet this part of the garden would remain all year, I would not have used the mondo grass there, yet it loves the almost mucky soil and shade. Small plants have sent out multiple runners, and the fat black berries sprout wherever they fall. Several nursery owners have noted this slow grower's rapid progress with interest, and their experimentation may help make this pricey plant more affordable.

These languid wood asters also keep company with several other late-blooming shade lovers. Tall, poppy-flowered Japanese anemones, *Anemone hupehensis* var. *japonica*, flower well into autumn, opening large, silky single or double blossoms in shades of pink and white above handsome, deeply lobed leaves. Happy in sun or shade, Japanese anemones are equally adaptable to damp or dry soils. They won't revel in outright muck, but mature plants accept extremely dry situations with panache. Indeed, you can see them all over the Northwest, growing lustily in reflected heat and utterly dry soil, the only fall flower left in long-abandoned gardens. They look a lot tidier when treated to decent soil and adequate water, which generosity they amply repay with more than matching return in the form of long and enthusiastic bloom. My own favorite is a semidouble white called 'Whirlwind'. It takes a few seasons to settle in, but once dug in it spreads and blooms with a vigor true to its heritage status. Compact, deep rose colored 'Pamina' is another irresistible sweetie that blooms until my November birthday and sometimes past it to grace the Thanksgiving table.

Asters

Japanese anemones

Toad lilies

Chrysanthemums

Black chervil

The anemone's gentle colors merge quietly with the soft lavenders and muted purples of toad lilies, *Tricyrtis hirta*. Despite their common name, these Japanese woodlanders are uncommonly good garden plants. The arching stems spread in slow thickets, bending to reveal the delicate, dappled, orchidlike flowers that cluster along the leaf internodes or in dainty sprays. *T. hirta* and its hybrids have creamy flowers freckled with purple or rose. Other toad lilies come in a wider range of colors, from pale yellow and buff to pink and lavender. They naturalize readily, and choice seedlings sometimes appear to delight the lucky gardener. Set these charmers close to the path edge, for their beauties are subtle and lost with distance.

If chrysanthemums are usually thought of as pot plants, that's largely because the nurseries are flooded each fall with sumptuous beauties in full bloom. Even if promptly planted, most of these will bloom themselves to death, passing away with the winter. However, chrysanthemums planted in spring will flower on schedule, then sail through cold spells without harm. One of my favorites is a deliciously pumpkin-colored *Chrysanthemum rubellum* called 'Mary Stoker', whose singing pink sister, 'Clara Curtis', is better known, perhaps because more brazen. Mary is exactly the tint of Italian terra rosa and makes a scintillating companion for bronze grasses and purple hazel bushes. A paler version, called 'Apricot', is also quite lovely in similar situations, and looks smashing with subfusc *Euphorbia dulcis* 'Chameleon'. Another pet is the small (two feet) but bushy button type called 'Bronze Elegance'. Its nubby little flowers are profuse and have a lovely, subtle color that blends with almost anything, from the fiery strands of blood grass (*Imperata cylindrica* 'Rubra') to the dusky lace of black chervil (*Anthriscus sylvestris* 'Ravenswing').

This last is an ardent self-sower that spreads its netted foliage throughout the garden in no time. Indeed, its willingness has earned it suspect status as a crop pest in some parts of the country, making it hard to find in nurseries. However, it comes easily from seed, which is still available. You will soon have all the plants you need, and can share the extras with friends. They are sure to want them, because this dark form is a fabulous blender, enhancing any partner with aplomb.

In my garden, the slugs enjoy the chrysanthemums as much as I do. Unless I am vigilant, the emerging buds are stripped of petals overnight. This sad fate also overtakes fall crocus like long-necked, lavender *Crocus zonatus* unless the gardener takes action. I bait selectively and with care, using pelletized bran and metaldehyde (Corry's), which is less generally toxic than most commercial baits. I used to bait with nearly empty beer bottles until I saw photographs of the garden looking like the aftermath of a really wild party.

Combinations that accentuate the strong, sculptural lines of each plant remain attractive well into fall. Set silky tufts of a gilded little grass, *Stipa tenuissima*, above sleek, swirling tussocks of tidy little striped *Carex morrowii* 'Fisher's Form', and both plants gain definition and clarity of form. The chestnut chevrons that mark the broad leaves of *Persicaria virginiana* (also sold as *Tovara*, or *Polygonum*) emphasize the vase shape of coppery *Carex filifera* and the darkening mass of tweedy *Sedum* 'Autumn Joy'.

As in any season, the essence of a good fall combination is that it please both the eye and the plants. Partnerships based on less fleeting qualities than flower color may hold their looks for two or three or even four seasons rather than a few weeks. Healthy plants, placed where their natural characteristics suit the gardener's plans, can contribute strongly for their entire lifespan. In fall, when many summery effects are in shambles, combinations with lasting qualities shine out undimmed. If these are in short supply, there is still plenty of time to create new ones to brighten the garden of the future. Plants tucked in place now may not look fantastic this year, but will be renewed and ready to perform next spring.

The Delights of Autumn Planting

 October

October is Flora's month, a time apart, when a gardener's every desire is anticipated and proffered freely. Each year, I am convinced that this autumn's leaves are burning brighter than ever. If some pleasures leave us languid and jaded, the blazing blitz of the fall foliage brings ever-increasing joy. As a child in New England, I remember walking through the woods, awestruck by the astonishing, piercing beauty of the trees. They seemed joyful themselves, their arms reaching heavenward in a praise song as lively as a gospel shout. Outstretched arms jiggling in sacred jollity, shaking in the spirit, immersed in merriment, they sing to those who have ears to hear such songs. I thought of autumn as a party for the trees, one for which they dressed with care, then stripped with the insouciant abandon of those called to an arboreal rapture, scattering the forest floor with brilliant bits of confetti.

Best of all are mild Octobers, when the rains have not yet returned in earnest and the persistent sunshine makes seasonal chores like dividing perennials and planting shrubs endlessly tempting. Some years, of course, the famous fall planting season consists chiefly of seriously wet work, performed rather crabbily to the steady beat of rain dripping off your hat and splatting noisily upon already sodden soil. This is when we gardeners learn whether we have the noble, character-building phlegm so admired by the English, or merely the gloopy, plebeian kind engendered by common cold or flu.

Wet or dry, autumn planting is generally considered to be all about shoving in quantities of dry bulbs rather than moving or introducing plants. However, as nurseryfolk are always trying to remind us, fall is an excellent time to establish practically everything, not just perennials but shrubs and trees as well. By October, despite a lingering Indian summer, the sun's heat is tempered by the obliquity of its angle. Well mulched and snugly insulated, garden soil still retains enough of summer's warmth that root growth is accelerated. Adding quantities of compost and rotted manure helps the process along, encouraging more fine feeder roots, which continue to nurture our plants even when snow covers the ground.

The silvery morning mists and drenching dews prevent our recent transplants from deadly desiccation, and brisk breezes mitigate the heavy, still humid heat of the afternoon sun. Though the brutal force of full summer heat is gone, there's enough of an edge left to sear newly exposed roots, so don't let new divisions or transplants linger too long out of the ground. Hustle them into their holes as quickly as if it were August, for the breeze can be as drying as the sun. Tuck them up to their necks in a fluffy blanket of mulch, but send them to sleep on an empty stomach. Overfeeding in fall can promote late leafing, which will be especially vulnerable to winter frostbite. It's fine to

Planting shrubs, trees, and perennials

Mulch

snuggle a handful of compost and aged manure around their necks like a woolly scarf, but nothing stronger is appropriate for the underaged. Long-established plants can have their compost and aged manure beefed up with alfalfa pellets or some seaweed and fish meal, but do bury them and cover well with more mulch, or every cat in the neighborhood will want some too.

When a cold winter threatens, the newcomers will be more vulnerable to frost than mature plants, so keep some big bags of mulch on hand to pile on generously should the temperature plummet.

Shredded bark is a classic, but mice are very apt to make themselves at home in adequately deep (eight- to twelve-inch) mulch, so add a serving of strongly scented naphtha-based mothballs or flakes along with the main mulch meal. I dislike shredded bark, which is always full of splinters, and far prefer to use chopped bracken ferns and shredded leaves, sometimes mixed with dried grass clippings. Any or all act as splendid insulators, as does salt hay or chopped straw. Large, whole leaves are to be avoided, since they tend to create sodden, smothering mats that choke out innocent little plants long before spring can buy them release. Small, fine-textured maple, alder, birch, dogwood, katsura, and hawthorn leaves can be used straight off the ground, so long as they are dry and can be loosely packed rather than laid on in dense wodges. The very worst are the leaves of bigleaf maples, which are worth using only where you want to eliminate the competition.

In recent years, the *Old Farmer's Almanac* has accurately predicted record snows for the Northwest. I can usually tell by the animals' coats, which get shaggier sooner when arctically cold weather is coming. If another hundred-year storm (which apparently arrives every three to five years — how time flies when you are getting mature) is in the offing, our gardens' deep mulch blankets will be supplemented by lots of the best natural insulation in the world.

That's if it's light, fluffy, dry snow, you understand. It won't be, of course, for when we do get snow in quantity, it tends to have the consistency of New York cheesecake. Now, heavy, sticky snow won't hurt our perennials, but it can play merry hell with woody plants like rhododendrons and daphnes and brooms, which are apt to be crushed to splinters when a neighboring doug fir suddenly sheds its load. Then too, any parts of woody plants that are not covered by snow are especially prone to damage, because the reflected light and heat can explode frozen leaves and stems, not to mention great, huge branches of towering cedars and whatnot. Ah, winter, dear season of quiet reflection . . .

The wise gardener will be hitting the fall white sales, stocking up on extra blankets to drape over frozen favorites. If you are of the Martha school of garden decoration, you will want to use flannel sheets, combining cheerful plaids with chipper solids. To keep them in place, try extra-wide ribbons in holiday red or tasteful hunter green. These will also add that finishing touch and mightily impress all the people who will stop by under the impression that you are holding an off-season yard sale.

But this is to look too far ahead, borrowing trouble from a winter yet unborn, which, old farmers not withstanding, could prove to be as mild as milk. In early fall, any gardener worthy of the name should be luxuriating in any available sunshine, performing chores at glacial speed in order to soak up every last bit of autumnal warmth. As we work, I suspect nearly all of us will take time out to revel in the intoxicating scent of lovely, warm soil, rich with compost. To me, enjoyment of soil is a hallmark of the born gardener. This appreciation for lowly substances like soil causes mirth amongst certain of our acquaintance, but I see it as a benison for the devoted followers of the goddess Flora. I mean, anybody with strong wrists can make lemonade from lemons, but it takes a true gardener to see compost in manure. It's a gift, my friends, a great gift.

NOVEMBER

November Cheer

November

Despite November's tendency toward frosts and drenching rains, the garden still offers a surprising number of handsome combinations. The winners are nearly always based on plants with a good deal of structural integrity, so their pleasing effects are due more to interesting partnerings of shape, foliage color, and texture than to sheer flower power. Though a little tired, these powerful pairings are clearly good at least a few more weeks.

My favorite involves a large, copper clump of *Carex plagellifera*, an upright New Zealand grass. This one fattened up over its first summer from a slim wisp of a plant (it was a scrawny gallon) into an elegantly waisted fountain. By early November its slim strands cascaded like water over its neighbors, veiling them in a shimmering curtain of rich, glittering brown. One neighbor is a mahogany-leaved coral bell, *Heuchera* 'Chocolate Ruffles', whose rounded, scalloped leaves have a rippling, lettuce leaf edge. Dark and glossy as the best Swiss bitter chocolate, they look good enough to eat, even in November.

The cocoa-colored coral bell is surrounded by a broad swath of creeping leadwort, *Ceratostigma plumbaginoides*. This tightly knitted, fine-textured little plant makes a pretty ground cover to interlace with minor bulbs at the edge of a border. Indeed, this spreading patch in my garden is threaded with snow crocus and May-blooming giant onions, *Allium christophii*. In fall, leadwort's tidy leaves turn hot crimson, setting off its starry blue flowers with brilliancy. In a dry year, the alliums' seed heads punctuate both the crimson carpet and the bronzed curtain of grass, their starry globes burnished to a dull golden brown. In a wet year, they sag like soggy and deflated tumbleweeds, creating a less successful if still weirdly compelling effect. (That's the kind where people can't stop staring at it and eventually push past you on the path, muttering, "I *have* to know what that is," then explaining sheepishly that they thought it was a dead animal.)

Behind the glittering grass curtain rises a fluffy mound of dusky green, studded with tufted little buttons of buff and beige. This is a famous old border chrysanthemum called 'Bronze Elegance', the favorite of the late Kevin Nicolay, botanical artist and gardener extraordinaire. Kevin gave me my first plants, and when I started this new garden, I sought out starts to grow in memoriam. Two small plants were set out about eighteen inches apart in April, from four-inch pots. They soon had grown together into a shrubby mass two feet high and dense enough to defeat the slugs, who elsewhere stripped the chrysanthemums of every bud. Though 'Bronze Elegance' doesn't begin to bloom until mid-September, it has staying power. Literally hundreds of the small flowers will have opened by November, with masses of buds yet unopened. Light frosts don't bother them a bit, and in a mild year, they will still be flowering at Christmas.

At the other end of the border, a hotter-colored group persists with equal vim. This one is based on a little grove of shrubby beautyberry, *Callicarpa bodinieri* var. *giraldii* 'Profusion'. Though its name is against it, its habits are all in its favor. Compact yet shaped with more character than regularity, this shrub has presence in every season. In autumn, its little lilac flowers fall away, leaving masses of tiny berries. No bigger than pinheads, they are so densely clustered along the stems that they look like fat little balls of some lustrous light purple gem, with the subdued glimmer of a semiprecious stone.

Beautyberry fruits best when planted in groups. It doesn't so much matter whether there are male or female plants as that there are lots; it's the party atmosphere that encourages a good show. Although bigger bunches encourage over-statement in the berry department, even an intimate get-together will bolster fruit produc-tion. Wherever two or more are gathered, the beautiful little berries appear in quantity. The shrub's own smoky autumn leaves emphasize the ripened berries' delightful tint, aided by a few choice companions. In my garden, the beautyberries are intermingled with obedient plant, *Physostegia virginiana*, a leggy eastern native with winning ways. Its slim spires bloom in several flavors, from vanilla to rasp-berry or strawberry sorbet. All of them can be manipulated like those little wire-cored dolls to stay in whatever position you prefer, tip tilted or kinked or kilted. I like them just fine growing whichever way they put themselves, but flower arrangers have great fun playing with this curiously adaptive plant. The varie-gated form (descriptively if unremarkably named 'Variegata') is an autumn showstopper. In summer, its long leaves are attractively marked with sage and cream, but in November

Carex plagellifera

Creeping leadwort

Chrysanthemum 'Bronze Elegance'

Beautyberry

Physostegia virginiana

Blood grass

Hypericum androsaemum 'Albury Purple'

Saxifraga fortunei 'Wada's Variety'

those gentle tints deepen to rose petal and crushed raspberry, while the lanky stems are topped with long spears of fuchsia pink flowers that echo and lift the softer purple of the beautyberries.

Beneath them are wide leaves of grass that ripple like ribbons, deepening from midnight green through ember black to sizzling flame red. Blood grass, *Imperata cylindrica* 'Red Baron', is a slow runner that looks best in colonies. Isolated plants look lost and inconsequent, but a small herd, moving purposefully across the border edge, reads most impressively. En masse, blood grass associ-ates well with both large perennials and with compact shrubby companions. In my garden vignette, bursts of blood grass swirl between staunchly vertical, rather sculptural clumps of rusty red *Sedum* 'Autumn Joy' and a stiffly sentinel brown grass, *Carex buchananii*. This last is quite different in form and texture from the weepy *C. plagellifera*, being utterly upright in character and remaining airy even in maturity. Its foliage has a rufous quality, and those thin, twirling leaves have a foxy red cast that brings out the pumpkin shades hidden in many purple leaves.

To take advantage of that revealing color quality, I often pair it with a shapely and beautiful burgundy-leaved shrub, *Hypericum androsaemum* 'Albury Purple'. Some sources carry a rust-prone form that is not a garden delight, but my plants are all offspring, whether by cutting or seed, of a plant brought from Albury Park by Edith Eddleman, a talented and visionary garden designer from North Carolina. Miss Edith's plants wouldn't dream of doing anything so tacky as to misbehave where they are guests. In all the years I have grown this plant, over several generations now, none has smirched her skirts with rust spots. If you have avoided this shrub, either for fear of rust or because you worry that *all* hypericums are relentless creepers (or creeps), relax and try again. Make an effort to locate a clean source and discover the delights of creating combinations with this colorist's dream, a plant that gets along well with everybody in the garden.

In my new garden, several Alburys are planted behind those ruddy perennials nestled under the lower branches of the beauty-berries. The dimmer purple of the hypericum's leaves is brightened by their wine red undersides, which flicker up with every breeze. That subdued yet glowing coloration is echoed by the final member of the grouping (it's getting to be quite a party, eh?). This is a fat little cushion called *Saxifraga fortunei* 'Wada's Variety'. Cousin to the common mother-of-thousands houseplant, this garden perennial has wide, rounded leaves that look almost succulent. Bronzy green on top, the fluting folds of the foliage reveal rich, pewtery red under-skirts. Between them rise long, red stalks tipped with panicles of frosty white flowers that open from September until hard frost. I also grow the straight species, *S. fortunei* ("Nobody's Favorite"). It's nice but not dazzling. The leaves are somewhat glossy but lack the luster of Wada's pick. (He is an incredible plantsman, so it's only fitting that plants named by or for him should be fabulous.) The ordinary species plant is larger, taller, rangier, and generally less refined than the choicer named plant.

Refined or rough-and-ready, such pictures cheer the sodden gardener, whose muddy knees and chilly fingers grow stiff the minute the warm sun is hidden by sliding clouds. However nasty the weather, our patient work of tidying and reorganizing without overzealously removing too much must continue apace, for as autumn glory drains away, winter's flowers are waiting in the wings, relying on us to set their stage.

Free Fall of Foliage

 November

As the juice and joy of summer drain slowly away, the garden is left with a new beauty, one that requires educated eyes to be appreciated. Bronzed and brown, slumping in graceful fatigue, the garden is drifting off to its gentle winter sleep. Tumbling in slow motion, pulled by the inexorable tug of gravity toward the embrace of mother earth, our plants move into their own autumn, bound in stumbling progress toward the next stage in the endless cycle of change and decay.

Gravity's tug calls the leaves down from the trees as persuasively as Hamelin's piper coaxed away the children. They fall in twos and tens and trillions, now fitfully floating like aimless birds on the wing, now cascading into fluffy drifts. When I was a child, I loved to play in the leaves, which filled the neighborhood yards in waist-high mounds and masses. Wading through them felt like entering another element, which I thought of (secretly, to avoid being laughed at) as dry water. Leaping into the leaves felt like swimming in a movable ocean. Burrowing into some great, head-high heap of them, I imagined how beavers might feel, snug in their nests below the water's surface.

I still love to watch them fall, twirling and spinning in private, ecstatic dervish dances or floating out in hesitant, fluting flight, curving through the air like tiny ships bound for enchantment. Follow them with your eye and you, too, could be transported, carried into the past or future, following the life cycle of a leaf on its journey through earth and sky. Fall's foliage free fall sets free the human spirit to travel alongside, wandering and drifting or swimming toward some desired goal.

This twilight of the garden has a magic of its own, touched both with melancholy and with the promise of renewal. Autumn is also the season when the garden's bones begin to be stripped bare, when strengths of design or lapses of balance are revealed. Should strengths be in short supply, we can amuse ourselves all winter by dreaming up ways to increase structural elements, introduce more powerful off-season performers, and create more harmonious arrangements of our plants. In the meantime, we can enjoy the marvelous mosaics created by our falling leaves, letting them linger wherever they are a visual asset, and removing only those large or sodden ones whose overly enthusiastic embrace might smother fragile plants.

Witch hazels

Flowering cherry

Scouler willow

(Purple) grape vine

Clematis

Potentilla nepalensis 'Miss Willmott'

Dogwood

In my garden, I am always trying to bolster the autumn display by adding shrubs that take on splendor as summer seeps away. A good deal of autumn's foliar richness comes from witch hazels (*Hamamelis*) and their relatives. This small family contains some of the choicest garden shrubs around, many with multiple seasons of beauty. Perhaps the best for little gardens is the southeastern native *Fothergilla gardenii* (three to four feet). Graceful any time, this twiggy shrub produces its honey-scented white bottlebrush blossoms in early spring, followed by big, rounded leaves that color intensely in fall. In November, these carpet my lawn with lustrous layers of cherry red, lightened by overtones of copper and orange. When still on the shrub, they make a volcanic backdrop for blue and purple asters and tawny chrysanthemums (which by late fall look a bit forlorn). There are a couple of fine named forms, including 'Blue Mist', whose big leaves have a blue bloom on them like the pewtery bloom on a ripe Concord grape. Roger Gossler of Gossler Farms Nursery (see "Resources," page 236) notes that the blue seems to increase with age, and I think so too—the first year, I could hardly see any difference between 'Blue Mist' and the straight species, but after four years, the blue cast was quite pronounced. Gossler Farms is the only source I know for another exceptional form named after the late Jane Platt, whose garden was and remains a treasure-house of choice plants, well placed and well maintained. 'Jane Platt' is the smallest fothergilla I know of, compact and slow growing enough to make it an excellent choice for tiny gardens. It also colors brilliantly and holds its color notably longer than the competition. A larger version, *F. major*, can reach nine feet in time and makes a splendid transition shrub between trees and open spaces or woodsy gardens and real woods. This species also has at least one particularly good form, called 'Suzanne'. Its leaves are faintly blue and take on vividly sunny tints in fall.

The long, tapered leaves of a flowering cherry, *Prunus serrulata* 'Ukon', add sizzling shades of persimmon, gamboge, and burnt orange to the lawn tapestry. This moderately sized (twenty- to thirty-foot), shapely tree also blooms in early spring, when its clusters of pale green flowers, lightly veined in burgundy, gleam against coppery new leaves. Beside it, our native scouler willow, *Salix scouleriana* (ten to twenty-five feet), sheds its slim, leathery leaves in showers of gold and hot Indian yellow. This one makes a large shrub or small tree, enlivening January with enormous pussies or catkins, silken and silvery. The clarion yellow is a remarkable foil for the candy-apple-red leaves of purple grapevine, *Vitis vinifera* 'Purpurea' (twelve to fifteen feet), a mannerly rambler that climbs trees and shrubs or rambles over the ground with equal goodwill. The burgundy-black young foliage of this vine looks especially dazzling threading between icy blue grasses like clumping *Elymus hispidus* (the best behaved of the Lyme grasses) or spiky hemispheres of steel blue oat grass, *Helictotrichon sempervirens*.

A hardy handful of persistent perennials are still blooming away this time of year, still giving of themselves unstintingly despite the first nip of frost. In my mother's Spokane garden, the last, bubbling blossom on sweet autumn clematis, *Clematis maximowicziana* — now, thank goodness, redesignated the more pronounceable *C. terniflora* — might be capped with soft puffs of snow. A sky blue scrambler with cloudy white eyes, long-armed *Geranium wallichianum* 'Buxton's Blue' enmeshes its neighbors in its casual embrace, weaving loose, lacy nets of light stems over every border companion. Its lovely leaves are softly spotted and marbled, often taking on gentle tints of autumnal red-gold that set off the white-throated, celestial blue flowers of a nearby 'Tie Dye' morning glory to perfection. In my garden, this geranium clambers into the lower branches of a candle-flame-colored ninebark, *Physocarpus opulifolius* 'Dart's Golden' (six to eight feet). This compact form of the eastern native shrub lights up the spring with its clear yellow leaves that dull to chartreuse in summer, then flame again in fall.

Nearby, a sprawling, recurving *Potentilla nepalensis* 'Miss Willmott' is in heavy rebloom in November, having already produced several flushes of black-eyed, salmon pink flowers through the summer. I shear back its sinuous stems every month or so all summer long, taking them back to within a foot of the crown. This triggers a new flush of strawberry-like leaves, quickly followed by fresh masses of pink buds. Both of these hard-working perennials glow hotly against a spectacular flowering dogwood, *Cornus florida* 'Cherokee Sunset' (twelve to eighteen feet). All summer, this shrub is decked with large, splashy leaves, chartreuse and golden, against which its dark red flowers and fruits gleam vividly. Come fall, the foliage takes on increasingly brilliant sunset colors until it rivals the most extravagant Remington paintings.

This season of change is a good one in which to introduce more exciting fall performers to our gardens. Although the year may be

RESOURCES

GOSSLER FARMS NURSERY
1200 WEAVER ROAD
SPRINGFIELD, OR 98478-9691
PHONE: 541/746-3922
FAX 541/744-7924
OPEN BY APPOINTMENT ONLY.

closing in, the garden need not die with it. By continuing to seek out plants that peak or hold their beauty during the darker, duller days, we can continually enrich the garden. If we ourselves remain alive to the garden's changes, even during the darkest days, we are ourselves renewed in its renewal.

Companionable Katsuras

 November

It's easy to fall in love with trees in the fall, when their blazing leaves light up the garden. In my new yard, a small Japanese maple turns scalding red, so intense a color that it stains the light that filters through the house windows. Throughout the neighborhood, the city, the state, summer green steadily gives way to copper and bronze, orange and gold, scarlet and crimson. The nurseries in November are full of enticing little trees just waiting for a home, many of them still taking on splendid tints as autumn matures.

Since most gardens are only big enough to hold one or two trees, it's extremely important to choose them with care. One of the saddest chores the garden maker faces is the removal of trees that were planted too close to the house. My new house is crowded by a flock of such trees, pressing against the windows and blocking our light. Although I've been avoiding the task, nearly all of them must come out, if only to make room for more appropriate replacements.

I hate cutting down living trees, but most of these are so damaged that they aren't much aesthetic loss. Set too close to the house and to one another, trees and shrubs never get the chance to develop their own distinctive shapes. Instead, crowded and misshapen, they are too often unhealthy, prey

237

to pests and diseases that ignore better situated plants in favor of stressed ones. Stuck under the eaves, which block the rain, their roots must go questing in search of adequate moisture. This causes competition problems with nearby plants and can lead to more intimate acquaintance with the Roto-Rooter man than the homeowner who planted those trees ever envisioned.

The lessons here are several. First, never, never, never plant willows anywhere near your septic lines. Not poplars, either. Got that? Good. Next on the list is to avoid planting anything in front of house windows that will ever surpass them in height. Have some trees, by all means, but position them well away from the house. Moreover, choose them with care, thinking of the future as well as the present, and not forgetting your neighbors, whose yards may be overlapped by your trees. Look for mannerly trees with multiple charms in several, if not all, seasons. Look above all for trees that won't outgrow their chosen space.

A park or arboretum is a fine place to start looking, for you will see what your selections look like as adults. Among my all-time top favorites are the Asian katsuras, *Cercidiphyllum japonicum* (eighteen to thirty feet), with leaves like little valentines. Heart shaped and curling, gilt-edged and golden or rosy and rimmed in smoke, they tumble in scented drifts about the garden.

One November weekend, while putting in the last few hundred bulbs (at least, I hoped they were the last—packages kept arriving with long-forgotten orders that I must have sent for in fits of spring madness), I noticed a piercing sweetness like milky caramel or butterscotch with a hint of cinnamon and nutmeg. It came from a maturing katsura some fifteen years old, which colors more quietly than its younger companions. Its creamy brown leaves spill like bronze medallions into the curling brown *Carex plagellifera* at its feet. Touched by warm afternoon sunlight, their spicy fragrance filled the garden.

Katsuras are astonishingly graceful trees, rising like slim flames when young, then spreading with maturity into billowy domes. In the wild, katsuras can achieve great heights, and in open landscapes they may reach forty to sixty feet, but in gardens they rarely exceed thirty feet. However handsome the sinuous skeleton and the glazed brownish gray bark, which grows attractively ragged in older specimens, foliage is their dominant beauty. Flushed with plum purple, the infant leaves are as decorative as blossoms. Rich bottle green in summer, they begin to take on autumnal tints in early fall. Their coloration can be exceptionally varied: My own garden holds several katsuras, as does my neighbor's, and no two of them share the same tints or the same time line. Some produce and drop their leaves early, while others trail weeks behind.

Choosing trees

Asian katsuras

'Pendulum'

'Pendula'

In the most open part of the garden, the katsura leaves turn shades of singing yellow and muted gold. On trees in slightly more shade, they are buff overlaid with salmon, coral flushed with rose, peach veined in old gold on red stems, or pale tangerine suffused with apricot and veined in lemon. One tree in dampish soil and little direct sun colors incandescently, the lower branches golden and the upper ones searing reds and oranges, veined in purple and stemmed in fuchsia. To enjoy them fully, we float them in bowls of water, for though their lovely confetti decorates the garden floor for weeks, they dry out and darken quickly indoors.

There are a couple of weeping katsuras, one of which remains fairly compact, making it suitable even for smaller gardens. *C. japonicum* 'Pendulum' tops out at around fifteen feet, making a round-headed, shaggy fountain of foliage that looks almost as beautiful when naked in winter as when fully clothed in summer. Its fine-textured leaves have a bluish tinge to them in summer but flame on in fall exactly like the upright forms. The other weeper is seldom seen in gardens, but it makes a bolder, bigger-scaled effect that looks splendidly dramatic in a larger setting. This one is called *C. magnificum* 'Pendula', and it really deserves the specific epithet, for it is indeed a magnificent sight. The only nursery I know that carries it is Gossler Farms (see "Resources," page 236).

Katsuras are choice small trees whose character improves with age. They are easygoing about company and work very well in mixed borders, where they can be interplanted with shrubs or underplanted with perennials. They can even be coaxed into carrying a small clematis, though it is utterly unnecessary. Even I, who am constitutionally unable to resist introducing clematis into everything upright, generally manage to keep my katsuras clean, simply because their lines are so good that adding a vine just makes for visual clutter. Trees and shrubs that are essentially indefinite in shape can take all manner of climbers into their arms, for such additions only increase the pleasing amplitude of the scene. Katsuras' shapes are so very lovely that it seems a shame to spoil them by adding anything at all.

On the other hand, that mature katsura in my new garden (the one that smells like warm caramel) holds a vine and it looks quite charming. Both had lived in a large pot for many years before being donated to this garden. Companions in captivity for many years, they are now companionably intertwined. Indeed, that clematis scrambled skyward at a remarkable pace, reaching fifteen feet the first season. It produces quantities of small, pale pink flowers all summer long. I'm not sure which clematis it is, and I would not have deliberately chosen a small-flowered, shell pink clematis, but the combination is extremely fetching and I am very glad it is there.

Best of all, their companionability means that you can plant a katsura fairly close to the house (meaning ten or fifteen feet away) and not regret its presence as the years go by. Indeed, you will increasingly delight in it, even if you should chance to have placed it near your septic system. Unless you put that katsura smack on the tank, you should have no reason whatsoever to regret your choice.

Hot Colors, Cool Plants

November

After especially hot summers, it's common to see
spectacular fall foliage. Even more splendid, however, are
summers when moments of heat alternate with cool, wet
periods. Though they don't make for the summer of our
dreams, they do encourage a larger amount of foliage sugar
storage than usual. These stored sugars create the hot reds
that inflame all kinds of leaves, from maples to sumacs, in
fall. The yellows and oranges that we see are really always
present, but are usually masked by the green of chlorophyll.
As the green drains away, the gold is revealed.

The result is a prolonged and glorious foliage display so
potent that even the garden perennials are affected. Hostas
bleach dreamily from blue to butterscotch, or from deep
green through shining yellow to dark shellac. Peony leaves
deepen to raspberry and rose or fade to salmon and apricot.
Balloon flower (*Platycodon*) foliage becomes a clear, singing
gold, and a host of hardy geraniums turn tawny orange or
amber streaked with a dozen hot pinks and reds.

One of my favorite near-black plants, *Euphorbia dulcis*
'Chameleon', makes a murky mound some two feet tall. Its
long, slim leaves are dull olive suffused with burgundy, their
backs brushed with pewtery purple. This once-rare plant is

such a prolific seeder that in a single season, its progeny scattered all over the garden. While the offspring remain darkly handsome into November, the original mother plant transforms herself into a sparkling heap of peach and biscuit, hot fuchsia and rosy pinks.

Maybe this is because Mom has been living in a pot for several years without a change of soil. She may be a bit starved, or she might have received more summer sun, or perhaps the pot provides better drainage than the clay in the borders. Whatever the reason, this plant has consistently colored well in autumn, starting a good month before her earthbound offspring. In a hot year, however, her coloration is outstanding, and many of her offspring could compete for Most Improved.

Before the shadowy 'Chameleon' showed up, plain old *E. dulcis* was grown chiefly for its autumn color. The straight species is a fairly dull green from spring through late summer, when it becomes abruptly incandescent and stays that way for weeks on end. A number of 'Chameleon' relatives also put on a good late fall show. The spurge family includes numerous members whose fall foliage is a reliably notable feature. In a good year, however, nearly all of the several dozen species in the garden actively vie for attention. Tall, shapely marsh spurge (*Euphorbia palustris*) becomes softly gilded, with burnished, coppery stems. The leaves of two Himalayan spurge forms, *E. griffithii* 'Dixter' and 'Fireglow', turn respectively terracotta and incandescent red, both on screaming pink stems.

A robust recent introduction, *E. schillingii*, stands closer to three feet than two, with broad flower heads on stout stems. This big guy is always good looking, but in the fall its eldest stems turn a smashing combination of sandy yellow, bronze, and pale orange. Its sunny tones are echoed by a clump of that indefatigable brown-eyed Susan, *Rudbeckia* 'Goldsturm', which might still be covered in bold, golden daisies after two frosts.

This is the perennial that a hundred garden books show partnered with tall grasses, usually *Miscanthus sinensis*. Though the partnership has become a horticultural cliché, it is still a potently effective one, largely because both plants remain sturdily architectural when the rest of the garden is drifting sleepily earthward. For a pleasant switch, try combining the more compact, rust and brown rudbeckia called 'Chocolate Shades' with the softer, silky little grass called *Stipa tenuissima*. As thready and delicate as the name suggests, this hairlike grass, when planted in small groups of five or so clumps, blends into a bewitching mass of green tipped with a palomino pale floss of fine-textured seed heads. Just under two feet tall, this tow-headed grass complements both the color and the structural massiveness of any of the rudbeckias, up to and including lusty old 'Goldsturm'. *Stipa tenuissima* appreciates a fairly open position, and its talents are wasted when crammed into tightly packed borders. Give it room to strut its stuff and it will charm everybody who passes by. The best planting I know of this bewitching little grass is in Linda Cochran's large tropicalismo border of hardy tropicals. There it has a whole small bed to itself, where each passing breeze ruffles its shimmering, wheat-colored stalks. Linda calls it her savannah, and rightly so, for planted like this, where it can run free under the hot sun, it reveals its wild, mane-tossing qualities.

Quite a lot of small border shrubs are reliable autumn performers, including the new sport of my old favorite, *Spiraea japonica* 'Goldflame'. Some years ago, it threw a dwarf sport called 'Magic Carpet'. This little charmer makes a compact cushion about a foot high, and in fall it turns the color of a ripe pumpkin. I have given mine both the obvious choice of partners (tall, bronzed *Carex buchananii*) and a less common grass, the ruddy, coppery, wide-bladed *Uncinea unciniata*. It isn't reliably hardy, but this tufty, tawny mophead is too enticing not to keep trying to persuade it to stick around for a while.

Certain of the hydrangeas color nearly as well as the azaleas, which are just passing their peak as November draws to an end. The best hydrangea for consistent fall color is probably the plump, modestly sized creature called 'Preziosa'. This means "precious" in

Euphorbia dulcis
'Chameleon'

Euphorbia
schillingii

Brown-eyed Susan

Stipa tenuissima

Spiraea
'Gold Flame'
'Magic Carpet'

Hydrangea
'Preziosa'

Italian, and it is quite a sweetie, with puffy little flower heads tinted in a gentle medley of pink and rose and soft purple against ruby leaves. The flower color lasts a long time before fading to muted French pastels in mauve and lavender and pale burgundy. 'Preziosa' has an appropriately scaled down version of the usual boldly rounded hydrangea leaf. In fall, the leaves start to droop a bit, turning marvelous shades of rust and red and old, battered bronze as they do so.

Interplanted with red-twigged dogwoods, 'Preziosa' hydrangeas provide a delightful interplay of color, form, and texture. Though both color nicely in fall, their best season may be winter, for the combination remains excitingly attractive even when the leaves are gone. Should we get a light fall of snow, the red twigs glow brilliantly against the white backdrop. Best of all, the hydrangeas bloom again, their battered brown flower heads gleaming with fluffy white snow flowers.

On Autumn Garden Making

 November

The fall color continues to be dazzling this month, despite drizzling rain and gusting winds. Perhaps this is one result of the ozone hole we experienced in May, when temperatures soared into the nineties. When the usual foliar golds and oranges are joined by hotter coppers and flaming reds, it's a sign that the leaves have stored more sugars than usual, a frequent consequence of extra heat. The birches and willows are ruddier this year, their typical clear gold warmed to bronze. The wild cherries have unaccustomed ripe-fruit tints that make gay vegetable confetti on the forest floor. Best of all are the blackberries, which are not just gilded but blazing. Mixed with hot lava red sumac, those long blackberry branches make stunning foliar arrangements, bringing a touch of the wild indoors.

I am especially aware of the leaves this year, since I am beginning a new garden. Every time I plant something, I tuck it in with a blanket of leaves, a freely offered natural mulch. Ordinarily, a damp November day might find me more inclined to read about gardening than to engage in it actively. This year, however, I find myself delighting in the way the chilly earth still softens beneath the light autumn

245

rains. Though cold to the hand, the soil feels rich and welcoming, ready to nurture and protect tender plant roots.

This is good, because somehow an enormous quantity of plants have appeared. As soon as a new garden space became available, the plants for it began to accumulate. Many were gifts from generous friends, including two nurserymen who between them provided enough to make an instant garden. When I was mourning my old garden and wondering when and where a new one would materialize, these gifts felt like a message of hope and encouragement. Now, they feel deliciously like work—the very best kind of work, demanding of one's full attention.

There is something incredibly erotic—in the true sense of the word—in the raw materials of any art. Nothing stimulates the flow of a gardener's creative juices like a having a large assortment of wonderful plants to draw upon. Wandering through a nursery bed or holding area reminds me of visiting toy stores before the holidays when I was a child. The sight of so many sparkling treasures sent luxurious shivers down my young spine.

It's the same with masses of plants, with the advantage that all this abundance is already mine to use. What's more, if I decide that empty southwest corner of the house is crying out for a winter jasmine, I can just go get one. The combination of freedom and power is intoxicating. Sometimes it's great to be a grownup.

Best of all, there is no post-holiday letdown with making a new garden. Indeed, the very opposite occurs, for gardens get more rewarding and beautiful with time. Well, maybe we do experience a twinge of doubt the first few times. When the enormous work of prepping the ground and planting hundreds of plants is done, the immediate result does tend to look like a sea of mud and sticks, particularly at this time of year.

Until you have experienced firsthand the way spring reawakens the slumbering garden, it requires a stretch of the imagination to believe it will happen. It will, though; just look closely at the sleepy plants and you will see signs of renewal even as they drift into their winter nap. All those bare-stemmed shrubs will leaf out next spring, because the buds are already in place. In some cases, they are already starting to swell in anticipation of the equinox that is still months away.

Our imaginations learn to swell as well, anticipating the return of light and warmth that will bring the garden back to life. When working in cold, soggy soil, it is easy to be a bit hurried and slipshod in our approach. When our fingers and noses are turning blue, it's not easy to concentrate on technique. It's best to limit the scope of what we do in cold weather, when a sudden downpour can alter our plans in a moment. Have all the supplies you need right at hand, so too many trips to the potting shed don't cut into the increasingly narrow window of planting opportunity.

If you have a sheltered area for storage, you can keep your garden cart loaded with a bag or bucket each of aged manure, compost, and sharp sand or grit. An empty bucket can hold garden scraps destined for the compost heap. A recycled plastic bag will contain anything that needs burning—whether noxious weeds, diseased plant parts, or unsavory animal byproducts. It's also wise to pack a bucket of water, especially if the season has been dry overall. It's amazing how often we come across a thirsty plant in the midst of a crowded border, or literally stumble over a dried-out pot where some languishing plant is trapped. Soak it well, then set it into the welcoming earth. It may look pretty sad now, but will very likely thank you with renewed strength and vigor when it reappears next year. I also always carry my Felco pruners and a hori-hori, that heavy iron knife that has all but replaced my trowel. I use it for digging out weeds, transplanting small plants, and dividing big ones. It's also great for cutting slugs in half, but that's another story.

So equipped, you can take advantage of any sun breaks as they occur. Even if you have only ten or fifteen minutes, it's worth it. Indeed, it's amazing how much work you can get through in such bits and pieces. When my children were small, I rarely found more than tiny snippets of time to spend in the garden. As I changed diapers and picked up blocks and washed endless loads of laundry, I

Autumn
gardening

dreamed about digging. When the precious, long-awaited time finally arrived, I knew exactly what I would do with it. That clarity and resolve didn't always make it out the door with me, and I quite often got sidetracked, but the refreshment was heartfelt, whether my exact goals were met or not.

Now that my boys are nearly grown, their needs rarely keep me out of the garden. They still require an astonishing amount of driving around, and they continue to generate an incredible amount of laundry, but then so do I, and we are about equally muddy most of the time. True, they eat like young horses and seem to unburden their sore hearts best in the middle of the night, when I am definitely not at the top of my form, but they no longer whine when I spend too much time outside. Even so, those long years when every moment of free time was hard earned have left me with a deep and lasting appreciation for the luxury of having time to spend as I choose. My daily schedule is not a light one, and down time is still scarce, even during the rare periods when I have nobody's needs to consider but my own. Too often, my garden time is snatched from other demands, my chores performed hastily and not always with the thoughtful care they deserve. Fortunately, this new garden was designed to be both giving and forgiving. Rewarding without eliciting guilt, it does fine without me when I can't be there, yet provides plenty of the work I like best. Those stolen moments have the savor of a secret love, and best of all they never lose their power. Even in November, the very briefest of garden visits have the ability to reawaken us to the subtle beauties of the waning year.

DECEMBER

Studying the Garden

 December

These frozen, chilly days of December are not exactly conducive to active gardening, yet I find myself prowling the grounds each morning, drinking in details. There isn't much to see in some ways: Long neglected, the garden is mostly battered grass punctuated by a few hardy shrubs. The wood's edge is tatty too, weedy and overgrown. On a frozen winter's day, the prospect is a bit bleak. It seems especially so when I recall the spilling riches offered by my old garden. There, on any day of the year, however bitter, something was in beauty. If there were no flowers, there were lingering fruits, or plants that displayed a season splendor of foliage, or marvelous line, or glowing bark.

Outwardly, this new garden is pretty sorry looking. The only signs of spring are the swelling buds on some tangled forsythia and a colony of spurge laurel, that most willing of the daphne clan. Lustrous and evergreen, *Daphne laureola* does look rather like a spurge, or euphorbia, with whorls of long leaves encircling tall, slim stems. Soon, the new year's thaws will coax its tight buds open, and their penetrating perfume will permeate the garden from late afternoon till night. Thanks to the fat fruits that follow its chartreuse trumpet flowers, this

European runaway has naturalized in the maritime Northwest, edging woods and meadows in bird-sown clusters.

That's where they are in this new garden, thickly edging the ragged woods. A few adventurous seedlings have begun a new colony beneath a magnificent redwood, *Sequoia sempervirens*. One of a pair, the pride of the property, this redwood had been choking to death, strangled by dozens of maple and alder saplings. Now its broad skirts have been cleared of all but the daphnes. When the ground is soft again, we'll add some creeping leatherleaf (*Mahonia repens*) and a few sword ferns from the woods. The idea is to create simple yet luxuriant plantings with the spare elegance of northwestern naturalistic gardens.

Planning this kind of improvement is easy, because the givens — the two redwoods — are so obvious. Elsewhere, however, it's taking time to figure out just what should happen. Learning a new garden does takes time — as much as a year to absorb the intricacies of light and wind patterns, as well as those of human use. Here, as anywhere, the first stages involved a lot of removal. Dead or dying or damaged trees and shrubs come out at once, clearing the clutter so that you can better assess the possibilities. Next comes the initial assessment, balancing assets against liabilities.

In this case, the wooded backdrop meant that the garden has an excellent tree line on three sides. Across the street, more woods will provide extended views once low walls and fences have been installed to screen out the road and neighboring homes. These barriers will also reduce road noise and dust, dividing the garden into a series of intimate enclosures, each with its own character and qualities.

Now, as I walk through the frozen yard, I see not just the icy stubble but ghostly groomed gardens. Those many hours of patient looking taught me how the tattered woods edge can best be edited to reveal its hidden beauties. Winter bareness shows us clearly where evergreen shrubs and trees are needed to reinforce inadequate perimeter plantings. It also points out strengths, such as plants that remain handsome despite the cold. Frosty mornings are as unkind to plants as to human faces. Anything that looks good now is definitely a keeper. (That's why this is a good time to cruise nurseries for reinforcements.)

Before any sweeping changes take place, a fair amount of both destruction and construction must happen. As experience has demonstrated, there is no point at all in starting garden beds where these messy processes will soon unfold. For now, it is enough to watch and remember, storing up details that will help shape those dream gardens waiting to be made.

Even if you are not contemplating sweeping changes, this is an excellent time to wander through the garden, observing what is there and thinking about what isn't but might be. This process is not critical in the sense of finding fault so much as an active exploration of the possibilities presented by any garden, emergent or mature. No matter what stage you or your garden has reached, change is necessarily the order of the day. Indeed, it is inevitable, and the wise gardener incorporates, rather than struggles against, the inexorable tide of change.

Happily, garden making allows plenty of room for change; indeed, it may be the most forgiving art form (or hobby, if you prefer to think of it that way) we can practice. When we make mistakes—as all of us do, time after time—our plants are very apt to recover without much harm. If they do die, as some inevitably do, they can nearly always be replaced, and the golden few that can't never wither in our imaginations but bloom on, perfect and immortal, in the ghostly gardens of Tir-nan-og. Even total disasters have their compensations, for the list of plants we want to grow is always larger than the available space, no matter how big the garden. The initial pang may be severe when great trees fall in windstorms or whole sections of border are flooded by torrential rains, but familiarity with natural cycles makes gardeners amazingly resilient. We may curse and rant and swear that never again will we lavish so much love on anything ephemeral, yet every spring sees us back in business, up to our

Daphne laureola

Contemplating changes in the garden

knees in manure, our heads full of seductive dreams.

My favorite time for garden review is between the dark end of the old year and the bright beginning of the new, the traditional time in which to examine the past and plan for the future. As the great seasonal tide of the year turns, plants and people alike feel the change. After the long night of the winter solstice passes, every day will be a few minutes longer. Buds begin to swell on shrub and tree, while underground, root and bulb start to stir. The return of the light brings a renewal of spirit to the gardener as well, reawakening our desire to create, to make, to achieve. Leaving the garden in slumberous peace, we can retire to a comfortable, well-lighted place to review our garden journal notes, old plans, and planting diagrams. We are looking not for shortcomings (many though there may be), nor for failures of accomplishment or intent, but for progress, however modest. Garden making is a lengthy process, one that lasts the lucky a lifetime, and there is no hurry about it but the natural impatience of the smitten to see plants bloom before they are even bought, let alone planted. Let's take this time not to carp about what remains undone, nor to criticize our own efforts, but to congratulate ourselves for whatever good our gardens have brought us this year.

Many of the gifts of the garden are easily listed: the long-awaited peony that finally bloomed its heart out, the roses that showered the grass with pastel petals, the lilies that spilled their perfume on the night air, the triumphant blaze of autumn color, the understated delights of lacy branch tracery against the pale winter sky. Other of its gifts are less obvious but even longer lasting—the glow of health that accompanies modest, pleasurable exercise, the lifting of the heart when a beloved blossom blooms just for us, the raising of our spirits when we lose our troubles in the garden's simple chores.

Bread and Water

December

Please pardon my slightly crabby attitude, but the holiday shopping season has barely begun, and I am already tired of looking at Stuff. Now, don't get me wrong; I love both the giving and the getting of presents. I have no trouble at all coming up with a list of wonderful things to share with friends and family during the holiday season. First, though, I need to complain a bit. What happened to the joy of giving? So many shops and catalogs that once enchanted are now rather irksome. Somehow, a relentless quality has crept in that robs gifting of some of its pleasure. More, bigger, better, rarer, only the very best. Gardeners, they assure us, need not just hand salve but honey hand salve. Not just any old honey, either; it must be special honey handmade by artisan beekeepers in exotic parts of the world. (Artisan bee-keepers? They must be artisans indeed if they are making honey by hand.)

Not long ago, one of my kids was sick. Too ill for school doesn't count for much, but he didn't even want to eat any-thing but bread and water. Poor baby, I thought, that sounds like punishment food. When I brought him some bread, how-ever, he said, "Not that kind, Mom. Could you get me a fresh Essential baguette? Oh, and some Cascadia water?" Huh.

There are a number of words to describe this syndrome, which underlies the glitzy, perfectionistic lifestyle movement of the past decade. The essence of it is that nothing ordinary is any good. The saddest part is that our appreciation for ordinary goodness is what makes life worth living. Devalue the ordinary and we condemn ourselves to that relentless striving after more-bigger-better. Like any addiction, this one is unfulfillable. What satisfied yesterday is not quite enough today.

I have always felt fortunate to be a gardener, because for us the world is constantly made new. Even in the dark of the year, each day brings changes. Leaves color and fall. Ferns unfold. Moss thickens and spreads. The green tips of bulbs emerge from the damp earth. Weeds grow, and as we remove them we find the buds of new leaves tightly clustered about dormant crowns, the promise of spring to come.

Even in winter, the garden welcomes and comforts us. Though flowers are few, each one that opens is a treasure to be savored. Even the flowerless twigs are not undecorated, for each holds a spangle of water, and each droplet is painted with a shifting reflection of the day. Maple seeds spread gauzy wings that also catch the rain, their subdued glitter brightening the dim corners of the garden.

Wrap up warmly and sit in the garden for even a few moments and its peace will become yours. Birds scuffle quietly in the fallen leaves. A pinecone drops amid a shower of emptied seed wrappers as a squirrel enjoys a meal. A dancing wind sets the branches bobbing, releasing the gathered rain in silvery showers. Should the sun break through, the air warms at once, offering a faint scent of damp earth and quietly growing green. Even when it's too cold to smell, the green grows on, however slowly.

Sitting in the garden, we find that restlessness falls away, replaced by slower thoughts and deeper awareness. In time, our breathing deepens as well, restoring our inner balance along with our perspective. Just being in the garden is a meditation, whether we mutter mantras or not. That said, what better gift to give somebody than the gift of a garden? A certificate offering assistance in making a new one or helping to refresh an older one would be equally prized by most of us. These days, time seems even more valuable than mere money, as do the companionship and benefits of experience that such a gift implies.

There are also dozens of Stuff gifts that are more practical than effete. Tops on my list would be a load of manure. Another antidote to the bigger-better syndrome might fit several friends on your list. It's an oatmeal-colored T-shirt that I've seen at several local stores. It's covered with little bees buzzing about and says simply, "just bee." Tucked in a gifty bee bag with some of Burt's beeswax lip balm and a couple of beeswax candles, it makes a happy and multiply useful present.

Gifts for gardeners

Oh, and some beeswax hand salve. After all, it really does help to soften weather-beaten hands and even removes pine pitch stains after wreath making. Burt's makes one called Farmer's Friend, produced cooperatively by ordinary bees and pleasant human beings. It may not be utterly exotic, but it's definitely good enough just the way it is.

O Xmas Tree, O Xmas Tree

December

It's the middle of the final month of the year, and you
don't have to be a gardener to be a little obsessed with
shapely trees just now. All the empty lots in town are suddenly full of trees with people circling them endlessly while
asking each other, "Wait, isn't this one more perfect than that
one?" Perfect? What does perfect have to do with it? What
we want is a tree we can love—for a little while, anyway. It
doesn't need to be perfect; indeed, that quality can be a liability. My oldest son tells me that in Japan, American
Christmas trees are all the rage. The Japanese trees are
apparently so well trimmed and groomed that they are "too
perfect." Ours, it seems, have more character.

The first tree I put up this year was full of character. It
was the top eight feet of a fairly funky-looking fir that was
crowding a magnificent sequoia. One of them had to go, and
it wasn't hard to choose. The bottom of that sad fir was a
ratty mess, but the top was handsome and decked with fir
cones. Hey, instant Christmas tree!

Since I don't yet own a proper tree saw, my friend Joe
climbed a ladder (under protest), armed with a pruning saw,
and cut off as much as would fit under my low 1950s ceil-
ings. Once removed from the embrace of the dogwood it

landed on, my now-little tree looked smaller and considerably less handsome, but it sure did have a lot of pretty cones on it.

This, perhaps, is the place to pass on my hottest tip of the season: Nothing removes pine pitch like butter. Really—it's amazing. Smear sap-sticky hands with a little butter. Rub it in well, then remove the whole icky mess with a paper towel. Don't go earthy here and use a real towel or you will be sorry. Remember the *Cat in the Hat* story about the stuff he cleaned out of the bathtub? Same idea. Transfer it to a paper towel and throw it away. Now observe, please, that your hands are totally free of sap. Apparently, the West Coast Indians used bear grease to remove pine sap after collecting pine nuts. This convinced me that California cuisine was as old as the hills, though I'm not sure what they did for balsamic vinegar . . .

Cats, kids, and Christmas trees

Anyway, we brought the shrinking tree into the house, where it somehow got smaller yet. We mounted it in the tree stand and tried to position it to best advantage, but there didn't seem to be one. I hoped my kids wouldn't notice this minor flaw, but they did. Actually, they were merciless.

My younger son announced solemnly that feeling sorry for the tree was making him depressed. The elder allowed that it was indeed kind of cute but only had seven branches. This, he felt, would significantly limit our ability to display our extensive ornament collection.

I, of course, said, "Nonsense," and made them help me trim it, which didn't take long. The result provoked one of those family scenes over which it is kindest to draw a veil of merciful oblivion. The upshot, of course, was that now we have two trees, one upstairs and one downstairs, in boy country. Because the upstairs one is in kitten country, we gave it the old baby-proof decorations used when the kids themselves posed a distinct threat to the tree's verticality.

Now, it seems, we are to have a third tree, but at least this one can stay outside. During our daily bakery visit, one of the kindly baristas remarked that he never liked killing trees for Christmas. I pointed out that tree farming is as worth supporting as any other kind. We don't mourn broccoli stumps or lily stems left when we enjoy the operative parts.

He agreed, but still wished he could have an outside tree. Well, of course there's nothing easier, I assured him. Indeed, it's great fun to deck a living tree with edible ornaments and then watch the recipients enjoy themselves.

Strings of popcorn and cranberries are appreciated by both birds and squirrels, as are many kinds of nuts. Peanut garlands can be threaded on bright ribbon with a big yarn needle. Trace holiday cookie cutters on cardboard, then cut the shapes. Spread with peanut butter and pressed into birdseed, they make swell decorations. Stale bread works too, but in a damp climate like ours, cardboard lasts longer.

I drove off happy, remembering how delightful bird trees can be. That's when the voice from the backseat piped up. "That sounds neat, Mom. Which tree shall we use?"

Well, okay, just this once. But I mean it: Three trees is my absolute limit.

The Gift of Light

 December

Anybody left limp or lazy or lonely by the holiday season
may benefit enormously from one more gift to start the year
off right. Though the solstice may be past and the tide of
light may have turned, it's still too early in late December to
feel much difference. If the dark of the year gets you down,
try giving yourself the gift of light.

In northern climes like ours, where it's dark by midafter-
noon in winter, many people get SAD. SAD, seasonal affective disorder, is a fancy way of saying we need more light.
For many people, bright light can change the quality of daily
life. It elevates low moods, stimulates serotonin production,
and promotes a feeling of well-being. Unfortunately, the
pearlescent, mystic gray light that envelops the Pacific
Northwest for many months of the year just doesn't cut it.
Some people travel to sunnier climes to get their hit of sunshine, but that is not always possible. There is, however,
hope for stay-at-homes: If you can't afford the Bahamas, try
a personal sunbeam.

I got mine from Discovery Bay Lighting (see "Resources,"
page 264). This Seattle firm makes portable light boxes that
simulate natural sunlight. The special bulbs and filters produce the intense light our bodies crave without excess heat

or glare. The special bulbs also minimize ultraviolet light waves, which are further filtered out to protect eyes and skin.

The bright light they put out is measured not by watts but by intensity, rated as "lux." On a winter evening, typical home lighting measures less than 100 lux, while a well-lit office in daytime might be 400 lux. Discovery Bay light boxes produce 10,000 lux at close range (which means within ten or twenty feet of the light source). Even if set a few feet away, the boxes offer a blissfully sunny experience.

The Sunbeam ($249) is the smaller model, measuring 4.5 by 10.5 by 18 inches. The more powerful Horizon ($299) is the same height and width, but 24 inches long. They come with a two-year warranty on the light fixture and a six-month guarantee on the bulbs, which can be replaced for less than $15 in either size.

How you use your light box depends on personal comfort and what you're doing. When reading or using the computer, I set my Sunbeam a few feet away, angled so that it bathes me in its warm glow without dazzling my eyes. How long you use your sunbeam will depend on your need; I prefer two or three fifteen-minute sessions, but the friend who introduced me to the Sunbeam uses hers whenever she reads in winter. Linda says her personal sunbeam makes her feel more cheerful and positive. For me, the light bath makes those gray-day blues fade away, replaced with the emotional lift I get from a sunny day and blue skies.

Before you invest, however, it's a good idea to check with your doctor and get a recommendation for a personal schedule of use. Some eye conditions can be irritated by bright lights, and some mood swings need more than light therapy. Not everybody needs a personal sunbeam, but if long, dim days drain away your energy, a light box might give you a boost.

Those of us who bring tender plants indoors for the winter might consider treating our plants to some light as well. Many of them struggle along all right without special lights but will do far better with a bit of encouragement. Linda also has a big sunporch where dozens of borderline-hardy plants huddle around a wood stove. From each corner of the room, a soft but powerful light beams down on them, and they look very happy about it.

The plant lamps are Wonderlites, a special wide-spectrum bulb that saturates plants with the blue, red, and far-red wavelengths that convincingly mimic natural light. These are the first wide-spectrum bulbs that can be used in regular incandescent light sockets, so you don't need special fittings or ballasts for them.

Most grow lights need to be set quite close to the plants, but Wonderlites are effective at a range of up to eight feet, and cast a fifteen-square-foot circle of light. Because they fit an ordinary socket, they can be used anywhere in the house. With their encouragement, dubious blooms all winter and red leaved banana trees produce new leaves in January.

The wide-spectrum light is especially good for orchids and other long bloomers, but may be of most use with large houseplants that are difficult to light adequately yet unobtrusively. A chart comes with each bulb, indicating optimal placement for a wide variety of leafy and flowering plants.

If you can't find Wonderlites locally, they are available by mail from Gardener's Supply Company (see "Resources," next page). Though pricey, the R40 reflector/flood bulbs last for ten thousand hours, with a one-year unconditional guarantee. The 160-watt self-ballasted bulb costs $49.95. A swiveler socket for $29.95 makes it adjustable to share the light among your plants.

Now, many of us have been perfectly happy with the results we get from ordinary, relatively inexpensive grow lights. So, one might reasonably ask, are the Wonderlights really different enough to merit their hefty price?

The experts down at Seattle's Indoor Sun Shoppe say probably not, except in certain circumstances. As spotlights, in dark corners,

Seasonal
Affective
Disorder

Light boxes
(for people)

Grow lights
(for plants)

they really do work very well. Where there is some natural light available and plants just need a boost, other, less expensive systems can work just as well. Indeed, these days there are quite a few wide-spectrum bulbs available that mimic natural daylight. For example, the Indoor Sun Shoppe carries a variety of bulbs that deliver light in a similar range, priced from $9.95 up. They say they can fix you up with a whole indoor system for a few hundred dollars, if need be.

Of course, plants are one thing, and people are another matter. Do high-lux lights really deliver the goods? For many of us, the answer appears to be yes. After some eight years of studies, light boxes are the preferred therapy for repeated winter depression.

January and February is the traditional trouble time, when seasonal affective disorder hits. Its main symptoms are fatigue and irritability, aching muscles and joints, craving for rich foods (primarily carbohydrates), and an overwhelming desire to sleep early and often.

Parents of young children will recognize this pattern immediately, but this is just another case of similar symptoms for different syndromes. In their case, the ideal treatment consists of sleep. Uninterrupted sleep. Unfortunately, the actual cure takes years, but don't worry, by the time the kids are sleeping through the night, you will be too.

> ### RESOURCES
>
> INDOOR SUN SHOPPE
> 911 NE 45TH
> SEATTLE, WA 98105
> 206/634-3727
>
> NOSAD
> PO BOX 40133
> WASHINGTON, DC 20016
>
> DISCOVERY BAY LIGHTING
> 11612 25TH AVENUE SOUTH
> SEATTLE, WA 98168
> 206/246-2996
> FAX: 206/246-0848
> E-MAIL: PAULT@WOLFNET.COM
>
> GARDENER'S SUPPLY COMPANY
> 128 INTERVALE ROAD
> BURLINGTON, VT 05401
> 802/660-3500

A recent study published in the *American Journal of Psychiatry* (August 1996 issue) found that there are two kinds of SAD. Simple SAD affects us in winter (and sometimes fall), with no spring or summer depression. Complex SAD can make you blue all year round, with the worst trouble in winter. If that's the case, a light box alone won't be enough.

A national support group for SADdies offers a lot more information on home treatments as well as medically guided therapies. If you or a friend suffer from SAD, you might want to contact NoSad for some friendly advice on SAD management.

INDEX

Ann Lovejoy is the author of numerous books on the art of gardening. They include *The Year in Bloom*, *The Border in Bloom*, *American Mixed Borders*, *Fragrance in Bloom*, *Further Along the Garden Path*, and *Cascadia*. She contributes articles to *Horticulture*, *The Seattle Post-Intelligencer*, and *House & Garden*. A recipient of the American Horticulture Society's Writing Award, she is the proprietress of Ann Lovejoy's Garden School. For a free sample of her monthly newsletter and class list, write or call: Ann Lovejoy's Garden School at The Sequoia Center, 9010 Miller Road, Bainbridge Island, WA 98110, (206) 780-6783.